THE UNION STEWARD'S
COMPLETE GUIDE

THE UNION STEWARD'S
COMPLETE GUIDE

A SURVIVAL MANUAL

FROM THE PUBLISHERS OF

STEWARD UPDATE NEWSLETTER

EDITED BY DAVID PROSTEN

Union Communication Services, Inc.

Washington, D.C. and Annapolis, MD.

 GCIU 629-M

Library of Congress Catalog Card Number: 97-61164
ISBN: 0-9659486-0-9

David Prosten is a member of Local 35, The Newspaper Guild, Communications Workers of America.

Union Communication Services, Inc., is a union shop, whose employees are members of Local 400, United Food and Commercial Workers.

Design and typesetting by Gerson Higgs Design, Washington, D.C. Carol Higgs is a member of Local 14200, Communications Workers of America.

Printed on paper produced by members of United Paperworkers International Union Locals 203 and 384, Moss Point, Mississippi (cover), and 265, 337, 1940 and 2650, Mobile, Alabama (inside pages), employees of International Paper Co.

Printed and bound in the United States of America by members of Graphic Communications International Union Locals 98C and 518M at Von Hoffmann Corporation, Eldridge, Iowa.
0 9 8 7 6 5 4 3
First Edition

This book is dedicated to the memory of
my father, Jesse Prosten, a good union man,
and to union activists everywhere,
who keep on fighting despite
so many reasons to walk away.

CONTENTS

This book is designed to help those who help: the hundreds of thousands of union stewards across North America who serve their co-workers and their unions by taking on the burdens of workplace leadership. Stewards are critical players in the success or failure of their unions. Unlike any other union leaders, they are in day-to-day contact with the membership and are in a unique position to be on top of what's going on in the workplace—whether the employer is abiding by the contract and whether the union is effectively responding to workplace problems.

To most workers, their steward *is* the union. The steward is the only union presence the workers see day to day, the only personal contact they have with the union unless—don't hold your breath—they come out to union meetings. In a very literal way, unions simply could not function without stewards.

This book will help those new to the stewards' ranks understand the vital importance of their mission and the basics of their role, and provide them with advice and counsel to make more manageable the demands on their skills, time and energy.

And it offers more experienced stewards the opportunity to learn new ways of handling old problems: different approaches, tactics and strategies that can help on everything from winning grievances to avoiding burnout.

The Union Steward's Complete Guide is based largely on material previously published in *Steward Update* newsletter, the bi-monthly education and training guide offered since 1989 by Union Communication Services of Washington, D.C. (For more information, see the last page of this book.) More than 1,000 local unions subscribe in bulk to the newsletter today and give copies to their stewards across the United States and Canada.

While the newsletter works to address Canadian issues in its pages—sometimes successfully, other times less so, given the peculiarities of U.S. and Canadian labor (or should we say *labour?*) laws—we decided that in this book we simply could not do our Canadian brothers and sisters full justice. Much of the matter in these pages does address concerns and situations that are universal across North America, but real differences do exist in many areas and should properly be discussed in a more Canada-specific forum.

Additionally, we hope readers will understand our occasional use of "he" or "she" when clearly the reference is to both sexes. It would be more accurate, in many contexts, to say "he or she," but it would also make it a real chore to wade through it all. You've got enough chores already.

Every steward faces different challenges. The steward's role in one union can be very different from that in another. Similarly, an experienced steward may handle routine problems and responsibilities without missing a beat, while a newly minted steward will have to build his or her response from scratch. Thus the book is divided into chapters and sections, some of which, depending on their own experience and circumstances, some readers may want to skip. Veterans might want to do no more than browse through Chapter 1, which deals with the basics of being a steward, or Chapter 2, which addresses grievance handling basics. Less experienced stewards, on the other hand, may want to focus initially on some rudimentary rules of the road before getting too deeply into, say, Chapter 3's discussion of the pros and cons of arbitration or Chapter 4's specifics on handling off-duty conduct or past-practice grievances.

Similarly, Chapter 5, dealing with job health and safety, contains information that addresses issues in a broad range of workplaces, and not every concern will resonate with every steward.

It would take the incredibly determined steward, indeed, to read this book cover to cover. There's an awful lot to digest, and a wiser approach might be to skim it for a sense of what it offers, then come back to it as the desire permits or circumstances require.

Readers will find that the chapters on grievance handling make up by far the largest part of the book. In many unions the steward is involved in grievance handling through several steps of the process; in other unions, stewards help in research and fact gathering, but the actual grievance is pursued by a chief steward or union staffer or officer. In every case, though, grievances and their handling take up a huge portion of a steward's time, and so a big chunk of this book is devoted to that topic.

We've tried to arrange the book in a logical order, with appropriate chapters following one another and sections within those chapters flowing in a way that makes sense. Some readers might find a different formation would have been a better way to go: they could well be correct. We gave it our best shot, given the wide range of steward concerns and the many topic overlaps that occur. Between chapter and section headings and the index at the back of the book, we hope you'll be able to zero in on exactly the information you need.

The goal of this book is to provide aid, comfort and tactical ammunition to the labor movement's front-line troops, its union stewards. We hope it will help strengthen the labor movement while it pursues its vital mission. Employers of all stripes are making things harder than ever these days for workers who are organizing and fighting to improve their lives. From the huge international conglomerate to the small independent operator looking to make his first million bucks, to the public employer who has decided contracting out is the road to taxpayer approval and thus re-election, the need for a strong, militant and united labor movement has never been more felt. Only unions stand between unfair employers and their workers, and without dedicated and trained stewards, unions cannot succeed.

ACKNOWLEDGMENTS

In the most literal sense, *The Union Steward's Complete Guide* could not have been published without the assistance of a great number of people. Foremost among them are the writers who have contributed to *Steward Update* newsletter since its founding in 1989. The work of many of these talented people will be found between the covers of this book, foremost among them Pat Thomas, whose articles comprise substantial portions of Chapters 1, 2 and 3 and all of chapter 7; George Hagglund, whose work forms nearly all of Chapter 4; and Jim Young, who is responsible for Chapter 5. Other writers who have contributed to this book, most of them with multiple articles spread throughout the volume, are Sue Dawson, Michael Mauer, Andy Banks, Tom Juravich, Kevin Conlon, Robert Schwartz, Kate Bronfenbrenner, Mary Lehman McDonald, Tom Israel, John Kretzschmar, Julie McCall, Tim Sears, Larry Cohen, Joel Rosenblit, Dvora Slavin, Tom Ruggieri, and Deborah Owens.

I owe a tremendous debt as well to all the other writers whose work has appeared in the newsletter over the years, especially Ken Germanson and Saul Schniderman.

Several people read the manuscript and offered helpful suggestions and much-appreciated constructive criticism: Brother Schniderman, Wally Malakoff, Phyllis Ohlemacher, Joe Brenner, Peter Goldberger, Sally Davies and Morty Miller.

The design of the book, as is the case with so many other of my projects, is the fine work of Carol Gerson Higgs, whose heart and soul are as good as her eye and hand.

My long-time associate, the eagle-eyed Lisa Platt, was, as always, a tremendous help throughout the many phases of the project.

Much credit goes to Alec Dubro, who wrestled the contents of several years' worth of *Steward Update*s to the ground, helping to organize the material for its transition from disparate newsletter articles to the book you now hold in your hands.

To Sarah Flynn I owe deep thanks and appreciation for being the editor's editor, using her tremendous skills and deep belief in the subject matter to help make this book the helpful tool I hope it will be.

To all these brothers and sisters I offer my sincerest gratitude. To the readers, I assure you that whatever errors of commission, omission, fact or presentation that appear here are my responsibility alone.

David Prosten

THE UNION STEWARD'S
COMPLETE GUIDE

1 A UNION STEWARD'S RULES OF THE ROAD

It makes no difference whether you're in your first day as a steward or your third decade, whether you were appointed by your local leadership or elected by your co-workers. You've got the job, and you've got a lot of people depending on you to protect their interests and defend the guarantees outlined in the union agreement. It's a tall order, but it's one handled daily by hundreds of thousands of people just like you, all across North America. Just as they survive it and even thrive on it, so can you. This chapter outlines some basic rules of the road that can help make that road a lot less bumpy than it might otherwise be. The new steward will definitely want to read them; the veteran might want to browse through them for an occasional refresher.

SURVIVAL 101: SOME STEWARD BASICS

Stewards face a variety of challenges: the mechanics of grievance handling; the wide variety of problems that members bring to them; dealing effectively with management; keeping in touch with the union's leadership.

It's easy to get overwhelmed. Keeping the following principles in mind, though, should help the new steward get through the first few months, and become an effective advocate for the union and the contract.

KEEP YOUR ENTHUSIASM

One of the first problems you'll encounter are co-workers who try to take away your enthusiasm. That could include the former steward, or people who have been around longer than you have, or sometimes just plain anti-union folks. They'll tell you how unimportant you are, that things never change, and that you're wasting your time.

All organizations, including unions, need new, caring people to keep them strong and growing. That's why you were appointed or elected. You have every right to be enthusiastic about your union and about being a steward. Don't let the naysayers discourage you before you've even started. Keep your enthusiasm, and in time you'll prove them wrong.

TAKE THE LONG VIEW

A good steward doesn't develop overnight. It's a process that takes time, and you'll have to learn to be patient.

Many new stewards oversell themselves. When someone comes to you with a problem, you may have to swallow your pride and admit that you don't know the answer, and that you'll get back to them. In the long run, if you really get back to people, and it's clear that you have done your homework, they'll have a lot more respect for you. Remember that your goal is to develop your skills over time, and in the process build respect from both your fellow workers and management.

ADOPT A LEARNING ATTITUDE

When you first become a steward, you have a lot to learn: the contract, past practices, the way your union and employer operate. All the confidence in the world can't make up for actually learning this information.

You aren't expected to know all the answers, but you must be the kind of person who enjoys finding them. Don't be afraid to ask questions, and *keep* asking them. Since you'll have the opportunity to learn a lot about people, work, unions and labor relations, that should appeal to you.

REMEMBER YOU'RE NOT ALONE

Depending on where you work, the physical layout of the workplace, and what shift you're on, you may feel isolated from other stewards and union officers. Always remember that while you may be physically isolated, you're part of a larger organization.

If you have questions or problems, don't be afraid to use the phone or visit an experienced steward or officer. Become known to the rest of the people in the union as somebody who asks when you don't know, rather than someone who tries to hide or bluff.

USE AN ORGANIZING APPROACH

Some stewards overemphasize the development of their own personal skills —trying to learn everything there is to be learned, trying to resolve all the problems themselves. The whole point of the trade union movement, though, is power in numbers—working with others to achieve common goals.

In addition to learning new skills, you must also teach skills to others and develop a strong and effective organization around you. Remember that one of the most important skills you can learn is the ability to organize and mobilize the members you represent.

WHAT IT TAKES: THE QUALITIES OF A GOOD STEWARD

You'll encounter all sorts in your steward work: new and long-time workers; men and women; workers of all colors, ages, ethnicities and sexual orientations; the scared worker, the malcontent, the poor worker, the good worker who's had bad breaks, the victimized, the bigot, the loudmouth.

You won't have all the answers for all their problems. You don't even have to like them all. But you must respect them and be able to deal with them at their own level. That means you'll take a different approach with the scared worker than you will with the workplace big mouth.

Patience and the ability to listen are key attributes for this work. Here are some of the other qualities you'll need.

WILLINGNESS TO DO THE RIGHT THING

The right thing is what benefits the union as a whole. Remember that the steward is the *union* steward, charged with the task of protecting the guarantees set forth in the union contract. The steward is only the agent for individual workers in terms of how they have been affected by an employer violation of the contract.

Since the right thing is not always the comfortable or popular thing—enforcing your contract's overtime language, for example—you need determination and some thick skin.

The right thing on occasion will include: arguing with supervisors or managers who get some kind of kick out of using their petty power by demeaning, provoking or intimidating you; explaining to a worker that his or her problem isn't a union grievance; or, because the law requires you to do so, defending the rights of a nonmember (in open-shop situations) or an anti-union member.

WILLINGNESS TO DEAL WITH BUREAUCRACY

The contract specifies procedures and timelines you must use. Management will have an additional set of procedures that they want used. Then there's Form A and Form B and Form XYZ.

And then this supervisor has to check with that supervisor who has to check with those supervisors . . . and get back to you.

This is probably the least palatable of your tasks. But you must be willing to learn to deal with red tape—with the goal of using it, cutting through it or going around it to the union's advantage.

A SENSE OF HUMOR

If you can't laugh at yourself, laugh at management and laugh with your co-workers, you won't survive a week. Remember to take the issues seriously, but not yourself.

But even the best-tempered steward runs into heavy weather. It comes with the territory. Time pressures, demands from other workers, bad-tempered and unreasonable supervisors—all these elements can combine to create tensions that make an air traffic controller's job look like a walk in the park.

But some kinds of stress are self-generated. Stewards may unconsciously create stress for themselves by trying to live up to unrealistic expectations about their role.

EXPECTATIONS VS. REALITY: KEEPING YOUR GOALS REALISTIC

It's unmet expectations that often make a steward feel confused and stressed out. Failed expectations can make stewards doubt themselves and their ability to do their job. That's why it's important to recognize some of the common misconceptions people may have about the steward's role.

You may not even be aware of the depth of these expectations, so let's take a little test. You're the only one who can grade it, so be as honest as you can.

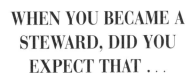

WHEN YOU BECAME A STEWARD, DID YOU EXPECT THAT . . .

☛ You would win every grievance you filed?

☛ Everybody would tell you what a great job you were doing as steward?

☛ The contract would not be very complicated?

☛ Other workers would rally behind you when you defended someone who was disciplined for poor performance?

☛ Being a steward would increase your appreciation of the basic goodness of people?

☛ You would achieve justice by fighting for workers who were always right against supervisors who were always wrong?

Sure, some of these expectations are a little overstated—but the point is that nearly every steward can identify with these feelings.

And that means that nearly every steward goes through the same kind of disillusionment. When things don't work out as you expected, it's not because you're a failure. Rather, you need to step back and look at the real world. See the box below for what usually happens to all those rosy expectations.

In fact, facing a few unpleasant realities head-on can actually make your job smoother and easier. It's just not possible to always be the knight who slays the dragon, and the sooner you realize that, the sooner you can begin working with the strengths you do have. Accept your limitations, acknowledge your mistakes and make a fresh start toward building a better working environment for yourself and the people you represent.

THE REALITY OF BEING A STEWARD

☛ No steward wins *every* grievance. Expect some losses and letdowns—and keep trying harder.

☛ If you ever hear one word of praise or thanks, count yourself lucky. Expect to be taken for granted, and be prepared to be your own best booster.

☛ Chances are your contract has lots of tricky spots. Don't expect to master it all at once—ask for help from other stewards and local union leaders.

☛ The union often has to defend people that nobody likes. People will ask you why you're helping people who are always in trouble. Be prepared to explain that the union is there for everyone—and that someday the person who's complaining may be in trouble himself.

☛ As a steward, you'll end up seeing people at their worst—when they've made bad mistakes and are in deep trouble. Expect to have your compassion and patience tested day after day—and try to understand and empathize with other people as much as you can.

☛ Hard as it may be to believe, the union doesn't have a lock on Truth and Justice. People, being human, make mistakes. You may have to admit to making a few mistakes yourself. But don't let a temporary setback discourage you from continuing the fight.

STEVE MAGNUSON

STEWARDS AS LEADERS

Armed with a realistic attitude about what you can expect as a steward, you can begin to exercise some of what every shop floor needs—worker leadership. Understand, though, that leadership can be a very mixed blessing.

A cartoon that usually draws knowing chuckles from stewards shows a flock of birds flying in a V-shaped formation. The lead bird is crashing into a flagpole while the other birds fly safely by on either side. The cartoon's title: "The Perils of Leadership."

Stewards are expected to be leaders, and sometimes this means no more than taking the heat so that others can continue on safely. But often being a good leader means a whole lot more, and has its rewards as well as its risks.

NO AUTOMATIC RESPECT

A new steward may assume that the title of steward automatically conveys a certain amount of respect. The new steward assumes that bosses will listen and other workers will show support—in short, a steward will acquire a kind of mantle of authority and importance.

As many stewards can testify, it doesn't always work that way. In fact, stewards may have to fight hard and long to win respect—not just from bosses, but from their co-workers as well.

Most worker challenges to your authority come from either a misunderstanding of your role or the high expectations that workers have of what stewards can accomplish. Some do believe that stewards can single-handedly create perpetual harmony and justice in the workplace.

To minimize these problems, work actively with the members. Before you handle a workplace problem with them, explain what they can expect from you—specifically what you can and cannot do.

Enlist their support in the action. Members can be asked to undertake tasks in investigation, grievance filing and bargaining, or to have a part in a meeting with management. People are less quick to challenge if they have been involved in the process, and it makes them better union members.

Listen carefully to the workers' challenges—some have kernels of truth in them even when they are delivered badly. You know you don't have all the answers, so invite the challenger to help in pursuing the solution. Keep workers informed. This may mean lots of repetition for you, but it's worth it. There are ways to get the union word out through telephone trees and workplace bulletins.

And don't try to do it alone. Enlist others to help you stand your ground against those people who are unconstructive challengers to your authority.

It also helps if you can carry some tested leadership principles with you as you try to work for respect.

HONESTY AND VISION

Good leaders tell a straight story even when they know the audience may not like the ending. Telling a worker that his or her grievance isn't really a grievance is one common example. It also means telling people that you just don't know . . . even though they may expect you to have all the answers. Good leaders don't have all the answers—but they take responsibility for trying to find them and involving others in the search.

Stewards should have an idea of what the workplace should be like and what it takes to make it that way. They don't get bogged down in microscopic details or distracted by petty things that can obscure the larger picture. This means looking at issues, concerns and events. It means asking, does this move us forward or backward?

LEVEL-HEADED, GOOD WORKERS

The most effective leaders are those who can keep their cool in pressure situations with both management and workers, and think before they speak. Certainly good leaders will show emotions—anger and compassion, for instance—but they know when and how to use their emotions wisely.

Additionally, good leaders realize what they *do* speaks volumes more than what they *say*. They honor the contract, put in a good day's work, work cooperatively on the job with co-workers and management, and don't seek any special favors because they are stewards.

LISTENING AND RESPECT

Listening is a basic skill, yet it's often missing from those in leadership positions. Good leaders not only listen to those who come to them, but seek out those who may be too timid to come forward. They also listen to those who have different views or who come from different backgrounds.

They listen to differing views without putting people down. They show genuine interest in others without being condescending. They thank all those who participate and encourage them to stay involved. They always speak well of their fellow workers in forums outside the workplace.

INVOLVING OTHERS—AND DEVELOPING OTHER LEADERS

Good leaders know they can't do it alone. They seek out others for help, ask others to carry out tasks, give others a chance to try something new and support them whether they succeed or fail.

They keep an eye open to spotting talent and give those people opportunities to take on responsibility. It may mean the leader lets someone else chair a meeting, distribute important information, attend a labor or community dinner, or write an article for the newsletter. They don't feel threatened by others who demonstrate leadership ability.

APPROPRIATE BEHAVIOR— AND COURAGE

There's a time to relax, wear your grubbies, swap stories and laugh it up. And there's a time for serious discussion, a no-nonsense appearance and approach. A good leader knows what is appropriate and effective with different audiences and different situations.

While good leaders don't shy away from taking responsibility for decisions and all that goes with them, they should not personalize either victory or defeat. Victory and defeat belong to the whole unit. Victory is a time for everyone to share in the moment, and to particularly credit those who had specific roles in it. Defeat is a time to lick the wounds and not point fingers, but to think about how we could do it better next time.

Good leaders are open to new experiences and new ways of doing things. They seek out ways to develop themselves personally and professionally through union and community training opportunities.

Developing good leadership abilities is a lifelong process, and stewards should approach it in that light. Building upon what you already know and do well is the best place to begin.

A STEWARD'S RESPONSIBILITIES: WHAT WORKERS CAN EXPECT FROM YOU

One of the perils of leadership is that people come to depend on you. If you're the union steward, they will come to you for all sorts of reasons.

They'll come to you to settle fights with co-workers. They'll come to you to complain about union dues. They'll come to you when their kid is in trouble. They'll come to you intimidated, angry, ashamed, disappointed, confused and sad.

HOW TO RESPOND

What do you do? What *can* you do? What should workers reasonably expect from you—the representative of the union in the workplace—based on their rights as union members?

It varies. These rights are often spelled out in a local union's constitution and bylaws and in labor law as well.

But basically, the union member has a right to be represented fairly by the union in all aspects of union activity—bargaining, grievance representation and internal union operations such as nomination and election of union officers.

ON A DAY-TO-DAY BASIS, WORKERS HAVE A RIGHT TO EXPECT THE UNION STEWARD TO:

☛ Listen to their concerns. This is the best service you can give a worker. Stewards can suggest appropriate times and places for this.

☛ Thoroughly investigate their concerns, be they grievances or other union matters. Stewards can and should involve the worker in the investigation process.

☛ Communicate information on union programs, services and contract benefits.

☛ Relay worker concerns and opinions to union leadership.

☛ Enforce the contract with the employer.

And in every encounter, workers have every right to be treated fairly and without discrimination based on race, sex, ethnic background or union membership. In open-shop situations, you must represent members and nonmembers in grievances. It's the law.

In reality, workers will come to you with both reasonable and unreasonable requests. In sorting these out, remember:

☛ You are not required to be an expert on everything. If a worker has technical questions about health benefits, for instance, it may make more sense for her to talk directly with someone from the health insurance provider whom the union recommends.

☛ You are the representative of the union, not the personal lawyer for an individual worker. Your activities as a steward should be driven by what is good for the entire bargaining unit you represent.

☛ Every worker complaint is not a grievance. A worker will pressure a steward to file a grievance because he feels wronged at the moment, but grievances should be filed only after an investigation determines that they are indeed legitimate.

☛ You don't have to be a trained counselor. Workers frequently bring personal problems to stewards because such problems affect their work. Stewards can handle the job part of it, for instance, if a worker is disciplined for too many absences because of a family problem. But you should refer the worker to a trained professional for help with the family problem itself. Your local union or the community service section of your central labor body can provide referrals.

A STEWARD'S TEN COMMANDMENTS

Regardless of the attitudes of others, you'll need to conduct yourself in a forthright and positive manner. That's why it helps to study some of the basic rules of stewardship—call them the Steward's Ten Commandments. Admittedly, these are *not* divinely inspired or written, but they deserve to be taken as gospel. They go like this.

1 Thou Shalt Love the Union and Show It

As steward, you are the day-to-day representative of the union. It may sound corny, but for most members, you *are* the union. You must speak consistently and constantly about your deep devotion for the union both in and outside of the workplace.

2 Thou Shalt Know Thyself

Be honest about your own strengths and weaknesses. Being an effective steward is a work in progress. What more do you need to learn? How do you deal with conflict? How do you best communicate with people? How can you be more effective in your role as steward?

3 Thou Shalt Be a Credible Employee

Follow the contract yourself and abide by the rules it sets forth in the workplace. Both management and the workers will be watching how you act to set the example of how they should act.

4 Thou Shalt Talk Straight with the Members

As a steward, you will be the bearer of both good and bad news. If you're straight with your members about what is going on, they will know that they should be straight with you.

5 Thou Shalt Size Up Thine Opposition and Act Accordingly

There's no one all-purpose way of dealing effectively with management. A good strategy involves a thorough assessment of management's strengths and weaknesses. Sometimes you should come on like gangbusters with them. Sometimes you should sit in the back row and watch them tear each other up. When your opposition comes from complaining union members—as it surely will from time to time—deal with them respectfully.

6 Thou Shalt Deal with Small Problems Before They Become Big Ones

Strive to settle problems before they become grievances. Strive to settle necessary grievances at the first step. Bring issues of concern to the members' attention when they first occur so you have a whole army of watchdogs alerted.

7 Thou Shalt Prepare Against Surprises

Surprises are great for birthdays, but they can be a real drag at grievance presentations, contract negotiations, meetings with the boss and your own union meetings. Prepare ahead of time for what will be said and done.

8 Thou Shalt Set Limits

A steward is not the slave of the membership. You will be expected to work long and hard and you will want to do so, but you have the right to set limits. It will make you more effective in the long run.

9 Thou Shalt Involve Others in the Work of the Union

The union steward is not a one-person show. The best stewards—the ones whose workplaces have really effective unions—involve others in all kinds of union work including investigating grievances, passing petitions, registering voters, attending labor and community actions, and working with unorganized workers.

10 Thou Must Recognize That Thy Worksite Is Just Part of the Whole

Stewards need to look beyond the problems of their worksite and become part of organizing on a larger scale for the improvement of workers' lives. This means that stewards need to be active in their community, in the political process and in other progressive causes and coalitions that organize and promote those improvements.

A STEWARD'S BILL OF RIGHTS

While stewards have responsibilities to the union and the members, the union and members have responsibilities to the steward as well. You have basic rights as a human being who has chosen—or perhaps been drafted—to take on an incredibly challenging role. Think of these as Human Rights for Stewards, although you may not want to take violations to the United Nations. But for your own sake, remember, you have the right to . . .

EDUCATION AND TRAINING

Your union should provide some way for you to get such training, even if it's informal.

GIVE AND RECEIVE CONSTRUCTIVE CRITICISM

You can't improve your performance unless you are given helpful direction. You can't improve your union unless you can offer it helpful direction.

AN ABUSE-FREE ENVIRONMENT

You are not guaranteeing yourself a peaceful life when you become a steward, but being a steward doesn't give anyone license to make verbal or physical attacks against you.

BE TREATED AS AN EQUAL BY MANAGEMENT WHEN PERFORMING UNION WORK

This is a legal right as well, but we all know how management is flouting labor law these days. This right is just basic decency and common sense. Some enlightened managements are finally realizing that it makes good business sense as well.

EXERCISE YOUR BEST JUDGMENT IN A SITUATION

Rare is the situation where the facts point to a clear-cut, unimpeachable decision. You have a right to make the call based on your best reading of the situation and shouldn't have to suffer endless second-guessing by others.

RECEIVE APPRECIATION FOR A JOB WELL DONE

Most stewards don't expect thanks and they don't get it. Isn't it time to reverse this chicken-or-egg pattern? The most effective local unions almost always have a system of showing appreciation for their stewards.

STEVE MAGNUSON

YOUR LEGAL RIGHTS

Along with all of a steward's rights and responsibilities come some privileges as well—privileges granted by law, and sometimes within the union's contract. This is because by its very nature, a union steward's job involves confrontation. On the workplace floor, in the supervisors' offices and in grievance meetings, stewards must defend the actions of employees and contest those of management. Often this can be done in a calm and straightforward manner, through quiet diplomacy. But you may sometimes feel compelled to raise your voice, argue forcefully, threaten job actions or emphasize the union's position in other vigorous ways.

Vigorous advocacy, however, conflicts with the usual management rules of employee conduct, which stress obedience to, and respect for, supervisors and managers. If stewards had to abide by these rules, they would face an impossible dilemma: either hold back when defending employees or risk almost certain discipline.

EQUALITY

In recognition of their dual capacities, the National Labor Relations Act and most other labor laws (both private and public sector) contain special rules for stewards and union officers.

Under the NLRA, stewards and union officers have a protected legal status. This means that when engaged in representational activities, stewards and union officers are considered to be equals with management. Behavior that could otherwise result in discipline must be tolerated. The National Labor Relations Board describes the equality rule this way: The relationship at a grievance meeting is not a "master-servant" relationship but a relationship between company advocates on one side and union advocates on the other side, engaged as equal opposing parties in litigation.

The equality rule is consistent with declarations of the United States Supreme Court, which has said that the National Labor Relations Act, the nation's primary labor law, protects "robust debate" and "gives a union license to use intemperate, abusive, or insulting language without fear of restraint or penalty if it believes such rhetoric to be an effective means to make its point."

The equality rule allows a steward to raise his voice, gesture, use "salty" language, challenge management's claims of truthfulness, threaten legal action or raise the possibility of group protests. Vigorous advocacy may not always be necessary, but when it is used, an employer cannot label it as insubordination and impose discipline.

The equality rule applies when a steward acts in his representational capacity. It does not apply when a steward acts in his individual capacity.

You are acting in your representational capacity when you investigate a grievance, request information, present a grievance or otherwise represent employees. You are acting in your individual capacity when you discuss your own work assignments, work performance or compliance with work rules. Being a steward does not mean you have a license to tell management off at all times and places.

LIMITS

The equality rule does not provide 100 percent equality. Employers may discipline stewards for representational conduct that (in the NLRB's words) is "outrageous" or "indefensible" and is "of such serious character as to render the employee unfit for further service." A steward may not use extreme profanity, racial epithets or threats of violence, and may not, under any circumstances, strike a supervisor. Nor do stewards enjoy legal protection if they organize slowdowns or work disruptions, lead contract-barred work stoppages or file grievances in bad faith.

However, the line between protected and unprotected conduct isn't precise—and

supervisors often exaggerate when describing a steward's behavior. To protect yourself, bring an employee or fellow union representative to grievance sessions or other meetings with management.

THE NO-REPRISAL RULE

The right to engage in concerted activities includes participation in grievance activities. A steward cannot be punished or threatened with punishment because management considers his grievances to be overly frequent, petty or offensively written. Nor may management threaten a steward with adverse consequences if the steward brings a grievance to a higher step.

Reprisals against stewards are unfair labor practices. An employer violates the no-reprisal rule if it:

- ☛ Unfairly gives a steward a bad evaluation.
- ☛ Denies a steward pay or promotion opportunities.
- ☛ Segregates a steward from other employees.
- ☛ Deprives a steward of overtime or other benefits.
- ☛ Enforces rules more strictly against a steward than other workers.
- ☛ Threatens a steward with physical harm or strikes a steward.

- Overly supervises a steward.
- Transfers a steward to a different job or shift.
- Gives a steward a poor reference for a prospective job.

THE SAME-STANDARDS RULE

Some supervisors take the attitude that stewards can be held to higher standards than other employees. "Of all people, you're supposed to know the rules" is often heard when a steward is penalized for coming in late or making an error. Other supervisors take the position that stewards are supposed to set examples for other employees.

These attitudes have no support in logic or in law. Stewards are not super-workers. Who would take the post if it meant higher work requirements or more severe discipline?

Employers must apply the same standards to stewards as they do to other employees. Employers violate the same-standards rule if they hold stewards to higher standards or impose more severe discipline for similar misconduct.

The only circumstance under U.S. labor law in which a steward may be held to a higher standard than a rank-and-file employee occurs when a no-strike clause in a union contract imposes affirmative duties

on union officials. For example, if a no-strike clause says that the union will "exert itself to bring about a quick termination of such violation," an employer may discipline union officers and stewards more severely than rank-and-filers for taking part in a mid-contract walkout.

Beware that even if a no-strike clause does not impose affirmative duties, a steward may be disciplined for instigating or leading a contract-barred work stoppage or slowdown.

In most cases involving discrimination against stewards, the union will be able to file a contract grievance as well as a labor board charge. The union should file with the labor board at the same time that it files its grievance.

JUST TESTING

Given your status, the amount of knowledge and the responsibility you must carry, it would seem that you're entitled to a whole lot of respect. But often, you find yourself defending not only your decisions and actions but your very authority.

Since management doesn't much like equals, especially when they are workers, that often explains the source of many a challenge. So does the management sport of "testing" stewards. Never assume a supervisor understands your role. Management doesn't necessarily train supervisors well on union rights and responsibilities.

If you are challenged by a supervisor, make it clear that you are acting in your official capacity as the union steward. Answer by keeping an even, professional tone. It leaves you room to raise your voice later if needed.

For example, you may say without apology, "As a union steward, I have a right to . . . see the personnel file of this worker . . . accompany a worker to a disciplinary meeting with a supervisor . . . investigate this grievance on work time according to the contract."

If a supervisor continues to give you grief, go over his or her head to the chief personnel officer.

MISTAKES TO AVOID

Because you have a right—indeed a need—to use your own best judgment means that you will make mistakes. No one avoids all mistakes, but that doesn't mean that you need to make *all* of them yourself. Here are some common ones to avoid.

It's a mistake to . . .

REPRESENT UNFAIRLY OR UNEQUALLY

Not only does it expose the union to legal action, it's just not the right thing to do. It undermines the whole purpose of the union and the very idea of union solidarity. Remember the old union motto: An injury to one is an injury to all.

MAKE BACKROOM DEALS

Management is notorious for trying to get stewards to trade grievances. "I'll let you have this case if you drop the one we talked about yesterday" is a favorite refrain. Every member deserves a fair shake and *every* grievance needs to be evaluated on its own merit. Never agree to anything with management that you would be uncomfortable telling your entire membership about.

PROMISE REMEDIES TOO QUICKLY

You are hurting both the member and your credibility if you pass judgment on a grievance prior to a thorough investigation. Only after you have spoken to the grievant and witnesses *and* consulted the contract and the employer's rules and past practices are you in a position to make that determination. Given the frequency of poor and mixed arbitration decisions, no steward should ever promise victory.

FAIL TO SPEAK WITH NEW WORKERS

The most important way a union gains the support of a new member or potential new member is by one-on-one contact with the steward. You not only want to provide the new workers with information, you need to build a personal relationship and begin to get them involved in union activities from their first day on the job.

FAIL TO ADHERE TO TIME LINES

Even the strongest, iron-clad case can be lost if you fail to follow the time line specified in your contract. Even if management agrees to an extension, it's not in the union's interest to let problems fester and grow. If you do get a formal extension of time limits, be sure to get it in writing.

LET GRIEVANCES GO UNFILED

Every grievance that goes unfiled undermines the contract that you struggled so hard to win. While most members see changes and problems only in terms of the impact on them, the *steward* needs to be able to understand a grievance's impact on the contract and the union as a whole.

MEET WITH MANAGEMENT ALONE

When you meet with management alone, suspicions may arise as to what kinds of deals you are making. It also allows management to lie or change its story. More important, when stewards meet with management alone, it takes away an opportunity for members to participate in the union and to understand that it's really *their* organization.

FAIL TO GET SETTLEMENTS IN WRITING

Just as you should protect yourself by not meeting with management alone, be sure to get grievance settlements in writing. Putting the settlement in writing helps clarify the issues and keeps management from backing down on its deal.

FAIL TO PUBLICIZE VICTORIES

Publicizing each and every victory is an important way to build your local union. This publicity not only has a chilling effect on the employer but helps educate your members about their contractual rights. It also gives you something to celebrate and helps you gain the courage to carry on.

FAIL TO ORGANIZE

Stewards are much more than grievance handlers. They're the local's mobilizers, who should be talkin' and fightin' union all the time. Each and every grievance and incident must be looked at in terms of how it can increase participation, build the union and create new leaders.

Part of becoming an effective steward is staying alert to what is happening around you. Stewards need to do more than simply respond to problems. They should be able to anticipate where and when problems may be brewing. Stewards also must be prepared to constantly reassess how they are doing. While it's impossible to come up with a complete list of all the things you need to watch out for, here are a few of the big ones.

In brief, you're in trouble when . . .

MEMBERS DON'T COME TO YOU WITH THEIR PROBLEMS

The folks you represent need to know that you are available and willing to help. Stewards sometimes make the mistake of wanting to deal only with legitimate grievances. Yet it is often through helping members on seemingly minor issues that you build credibility and respect that is invaluable in solving more serious problems. Be sure to publicize your union's grievance victories on the union bulletin board or a regular newsletter to remind members of what can be won through grievances and union representation.

MEMBERS SEEK HELP FROM OTHER STEWARDS

This may be happening because you haven't been making yourself available, but it sometimes occurs when stewards are new or inexperienced. To get more experience you should take advantage of whatever steward training programs the union offers and you should regularly seek the advice of more experienced stewards. Another reason members may not be seeking you out: rightly or wrongly, they may perceive that you are tied to a particular clique or group of workers. You must make it clear to all of the members that you have no favorites and are prepared to represent everyone equally.

MANAGEMENT REFUSES TO MEET WITH YOU

You have to build credibility with management, not just the members. This is not to suggest that management will always like you, but through your integrity, persistence and hard work, management will realize that you are a force they need to contend with.

MEMBERS AND MANAGEMENT MAKE PRIVATE DEALS WITHOUT YOUR OR THE UNION'S INVOLVEMENT

You need to make members understand that without the assistance of a steward and the union, the likelihood of getting justice is very small. Furthermore, without the involvement of the union, these backroom deals frequently undermine the contract and in the long run make things worse for everybody.

YOU NEVER WIN A GRIEVANCE

Winning isn't everything, particularly if you're up against an aggressive employer or in a difficult workplace. But if you are only rarely winning it's time to reevaluate your grievance strategy. Are you filing too many grievances that don't have merit? Are you doing thorough grievance investigations? Are you carefully preparing for the hearing, including practicing with the grievant and witnesses? Are you figuring ways to pressure the employer outside the grievance procedure? Maybe this is a good time for a grievance refresher course. It also may be a good time to do some internal organizing in order to use rank-and-file support to pressure the employer to settle in the union's favor.

YOU MISS UNION MEETINGS

We're all busy and it's not always easy juggling everything. But being an effective steward is not just handling problems in your department or section. You need to be an active union member and up to date on what is happening in the rest of the local.

You also need to attend meetings to make sure that the interests and concerns of the members you represent are heard and addressed by the local union.

YOU HEAR DECERTIFICATION RUMORS

While members may sometimes threaten to get rid of the union if they don't win a grievance or get things their way, this is not something to kid around with. Your brother and sister workers and maybe you, too, fought hard to get your union, and everything you gained can be wiped out in one decertification election. The best way to prevent and defuse decertification is to launch an internal organizing drive addressing the issues and concerns that are most important to your members. But don't try to handle this all by yourself. These decertification campaigns sometimes gather far too much momentum before the union becomes aware, so report any activity to the officers of the local as soon as possible.

2 GRIEVANCE BASICS: YOUR FIRST MOVES

While different unions deal with grievance handling in different ways, it's the rare union in which the steward is not playing a role, usually a key role, in the process.

In some unions the steward fields the initial complaint, does the basic investigation, then alerts a union officer or professional union staffer to the problem and steps back to let the higher-up carry the ball.

In other unions the steward pursues the grievance through its first or second or even third step before passing it up to a chief steward or other union official for further handling, if still unresolved. The steward in these cases can find herself knee-deep in investigations, paperwork and meetings.

While stewards' degrees of involvement may vary based on their own union's practices and procedures, handling co-workers' grievances is at the core of the work. There are certain basics that every activist should know about the process, and it's the goal of this chapter to give a rundown on the ABCs.

Stewards learn quickly that like so many other things in this world, grievances are not always what they seem.

Often, a worker brings a steward a grievance that's clearly an out-and-out violation of rights. At other times, it's impossible to tell whether a complaint is actually a grievance until it has been thoroughly investigated. In still other cases, a steward knows right off the bat that what's needed is some serious personal counseling, not a grievance against the boss.

Stewards who investigate charges that arise in the grievance process often find that first impressions can be wrong. People don't tell the truth, or the truth is hard to uncover. The contract doesn't say what everyone assumes it says. In some cases the problem may be no big deal to management and can be remedied with a friendly suggestion.

Half the grievants who come in will tell a steward—and anyone else they can find—that they're taking this one to the highest court in the land. They want the world to know they've been wronged. They want justice. They want the guilty parties punished.

But it's usually the steward's job to see that the issue is resolved not with the most noise and effort but with the least. If there's one golden rule you need to know about most grievances, it's this: settle them at the lowest level possible. And if it isn't a grievance, let the member know as soon as you realize that's the case.

IS IT REALLY A GRIEVANCE?

Stewards generally agree that the term *grievance* is the most misunderstood word in the workplace. Some workers believe that anything they don't like about work is a grievance. Other workers endure flagrant violations of their legal rights by management but shy away from the word.

So how do workers know when they have a grievance?

While some contracts actually define the word, broadly speaking, a grievance is a violation of worker rights. The steward needs to know (a) what those rights are and (b) if they have indeed been violated. This is rarely an easy process.

The first step is to conduct a thorough investigation of the incident or situation. That includes interviewing the worker, the supervisor and any witnesses. It can also include checking records or requesting written information from management, and perhaps from the worker as well.

Once the investigation is complete, the steward can examine the information to determine if there is truly a grievance. The vast majority of grievances fall into the following categories.

VIOLATION OF THE CONTRACT

Contract violations involve such matters as wages, hours, working conditions, vacations, holidays and benefits. The contract also usually spells out disciplinary actions and procedures.

If management has violated something spelled out in the contract, the union can file a grievance. For example, say your contract specifies that a worker should receive time and a half for more than eight hours' work in a day. If a worker is denied that overtime pay, you have grounds for a grievance.

VIOLATION OF PAST PRACTICE

No contract spells out every practice on the job. A practice that has been in place for an extended period of time and is accepted by both the union and management explicitly (verbally or in writing) or implicitly (neither side has ever objected) can be the basis for a grievance if it is violated.

The classic example is wash-up time, a practice in many industrial settings where workers use the last ten or fifteen minutes before the end of the shift to clean up. Nothing in the contract specifies wash-up time, but it's an accepted practice. If a worker washing up suddenly gets disciplined for not being on the job, the union could file a past-practice grievance.

VIOLATION OF FAIR TREATMENT

If management discriminates on the basis of race, sex, nationality, religion or union activity, the union can file a grievance based on unfair treatment. If a supervisor consistently gives all the dangerous or dirty work to a worker because he is Asian, for instance, that could constitute grounds for a violation-of-fair-treatment grievance.

Grievances of this nature are difficult to prove but important to pursue. Stewards should ask victimized workers to keep a little notebook handy and write down what was done and said, complete with dates, places and witnesses.

VIOLATION OF FEDERAL, STATE OR LOCAL LAW

Laws written to protect workers are considered part of the contract and a violation of such a law can constitute a grievance. Such laws include the Fair Labor Standards Act (FLSA) and the Occupational Safety and Health Act (OSHA).

VIOLATION OF MANAGEMENT'S RULES OR RESPONSIBILITIES

Management has certain responsibilities it must carry out. Most managements also set additional policies in accordance with the contract. If management fails to fulfill its responsibilities or breaks its own policies, it may be the basis for a grievance.

Say management has a policy prohibiting alcoholic refreshments at parties at the workplace. A supervisor throws a birthday party for his secretary, invites other workers and serves champagne. A worker who attends later gets disciplined by another supervisor. This would constitute a grievance under this standard because management broke its own rules.

SAYING "NO" TO A GRIEVANT

There are plenty of times when there's a real problem, but it's not with the contract or management—it's with the grievant. Most stewards say the toughest task is dealing with members who believe they have a legitimate grievance, but investigation shows they really don't.

If you determine that a worker's problem is not a grievance, you've also probably found that what happened was truly unfair to the worker, but it's not covered by the current contract or past practice; or what happened had more involved in it than the worker reported, and the worker's actions—in full or in part—contributed to the problem.

In either case, you have to talk with the worker. You have to discuss the results of your investigation; make it clear that the problem is not a grievance, and why it is not; and offer suggestions for resolving the problem.

Be prepared for the worker's strong emotions. Put yourself in his shoes. He feels wronged, victimized, possibly angry, frightened or demeaned. And when informed that it's not a grievance, he is likely also to be angry or frustrated at you and at the union.

It can be hard to say no, but there are ways to make the experience less painful for everyone concerned.

DON'T PUT IT OFF

It's natural to want to put off delivering bad news. But as soon as you have determined that the problem is not a grievance, it's best to tell the worker. By responding in a timely way you'll convey that the union took the worker's problem seriously enough to investigate it promptly.

MAKE SURE THE WORKER IS THE FIRST TO KNOW

Other workers may know about the worker's problem and will be curious to know what the union is going to do. Be sure to talk to the worker first before you have a discussion about the issue with others. It shows the union's respect for the worker.

EXPLAIN THE ISSUE FULLY

Choose a time when both you and the worker can talk without interruptions. Go over the criteria for determining a grievance and explain why the problem does not meet the criteria. Show the parts of the contract or personnel rules that may be pertinent to the issue but do not address it fully. If the union has faced the problem before, discuss the background and what happened.

ACKNOWLEDGE THE WORKER'S FEELINGS

Faced with this news, a worker may react with fear, sadness or anger: maybe directed at you, maybe directed at the union, or (not often enough) even the employer. As long as the abuse isn't directed toward you, allow the worker an opportunity to express his feelings. Tell how you understand that it's upsetting.

EXPLAIN THE PITFALLS OF FILING GRIEVANCES ON NONGRIEVABLE ISSUES

Many workers do not understand that the union will lose credibility with both its members and management if it files frivolous, impossible-to-win grievances. Doing so can undermine the union's ability to bargain and handle legitimate grievances. It can lead to petty retaliation from management. Point out that the time spent fighting a losing battle could be better used to work on the issue in a more meaningful way.

OFFER TO HELP IN OTHER WAYS

If the worker has a legitimate problem, filing a grievance is only one way to deal with it. Offer to go with the worker to the supervisor and have an informal discussion. Enlist the worker to find out if others have experienced the same problem. Ask the worker to relate his experience at the next union meeting or to the bargaining committee so others are aware and can come up with ideas on how the union can address the problem.

If the worker's problem is a personal difficulty—for example, domestic problems or disrupted child care arrangements—refer him to an employee assistance counselor, if possible, or to the community services offered through many central labor councils.

USE THE OPPORTUNITY TO INVOLVE THE WORKER IN THE UNION

Through your attention and by offering other ways to help the worker, you have shown that the union cares. You've created an opportunity to say, "We'd like your help on this issue so that the next time someone has a problem, we'll be in an even stronger position to address it."

Such discussions require tact. The most important quality to get across is direct and honest concern. The union cares about the issue and wants to help the worker resolve it. But the steward should not make promises to the worker about taking action on the situation if action isn't warranted or prudent at the time. You should explain the consequences of filing grievances that aren't legitimate.

Even after such discussions, some workers will leave angry. Some will stay angry, while others will come to see the union's point of view. What's more important here is that others in the unit see that the union takes the contract seriously, and takes worker concerns and problems seriously, but doesn't undermine its responsibility or credibility by pursuing frivolous or nonlegitimate grievances. It also sends a message to management that the union takes its responsibility seriously.

Don't let a bad reaction get you down. Experienced stewards know being a steward means you can't please everyone.

GRIEVANCE INTERVIEWING SKILLS

Workers bring all kinds of problems and concerns to their union stewards, and an issue isn't always cut and dried. Often, it's only through effective interviewing and investigation that the steward can get all the information and facts needed to totally understand and work out a solution to the problem.

Stewards know that the key to good interviewing skills is the process of getting information by using the Five W's:

Who is the worker?
(the basics of name, job title, employee number, shift, seniority, etc.). *Who* witnessed the incident or was involved in the situation? *Who* are the management people involved?

What happened or failed to happen?
What did the worker(s) do? *What* did management say, do or fail to do? *What's* happened in the past? *What* should be done? (the remedy)

When did the incident happen?
(date, time)

Where did the incident happen?
(location)

Why is this incident a grievance?
Why did the incident happen? (this question often generates more opinion than fact, but it *is* important)

Stewards new to interviewing often find it useful to write these questions out ahead of time and have them in hand when doing the interview. Stewards should make notes during interviews; there may even be some type of grievance interview form available from the union.

Experienced stewards know that a good interview goes beyond a "just the facts, ma'am" encounter. It's a two-way communication that collects information, demonstrates the union's concern and involves the worker in beginning to analyze the issue.

Here are some tips to make your interviews as effective as possible:

- ☛ **Choose the right place and time for the interview.** A convenient, quiet place when you're not both rushed is best.
- ☛ *Actively* **listen.** Encourage the worker to talk freely—it's important for a

worker to vent feelings initially. Convey a friendly and attentive attitude. Say little except to make good use of phrases such as "I understand" and "Could you tell me more?"

☛ **Direct the interview**. Once the worker's feelings are out, tactfully steer the conversation to what you still need to know. Build on what the worker has already said by repeating her own phrases. This technique indicates that you listened well and would like her to talk more about that area. Example: Worker says, "My supervisor was always checking up on me." Steward asks, "You say your supervisor was always checking on you?" and waits for more.

☛ **Weigh alternatives**. Once you've heard the feelings and obtained the facts, together with the worker you may want to probe solutions for some problems. Even though you have ideas, ask the worker what she thinks should be done. Examine suggested solutions with the worker by asking, "What effect would that action have on you, on your supervisor or on your co-workers?"

You may succeed in having the worker solve the problem or develop an action plan that's truly her own. That's a much more satisfying and empowering experience than solving the problem *for* the worker.

TAKING GOOD NOTES

A steward in a training session was asked how he knew that the notes he took were good. "They're good notes," he replied, "because I can find them when I need them later and I can read my own writing!"

Like just showing up for life, taking notes in the first place, keeping them, and being able to read them when you need them is 80 percent of the game. There are a number of reasons why notes are essential:

☛ You won't remember all you hear by the time you need to use it for writing the grievance or arguing your case.

☛ A written record can be used by others in the union (the chief steward, a union representative or a union attorney) who may handle grievances at later steps or in arbitration.

☛ A written record helps you compare conflicting accounts of the same situation. It's not uncommon for the grievant to tell you one version of the incident and the supervisor another.

☞ Writing down what people tell you demonstrates to them that you take your responsibilities as steward seriously and that the union cares. Your notes can also be used as evidence that you conducted an investigation if a worker later claims that the union failed to fairly represent him or her.

☞ Note-taking forces you to organize your interview more effectively and helps you be more thorough.

In order to make the process easier:

☞ If the union has a grievance interviewing form, make sure you use it. If not, write out the Five W's and other relevant questions before the interview. Leave space for answers.

☞ Ask the interviewee to repeat information so you can write it accurately. Let him know that the notes are for "union eyes only."

☞ Try to get direct quotes on what the interviewee says was said and use quotation marks to indicate direct quotes in your notes. For example: According to Ralph, when Ralph called in sick, the supervisor said,

"You're a bald-faced liar." Ralph replied, "Those are fighting words."

☞ When you are finished with the interview, go over your notes with the interviewee to make sure you have written everything accurately. Again, this conveys to the worker that the union is interested in being accurate.

☞ When in doubt, write it down. People will give you all kinds of information during interviews and some of it you really won't need. But it's more efficient to take it down at the time than to have to go back again when memories get fuzzy.

As you become more experienced with the grievance process, you will have a better idea of the information you'll need and note-taking will become easier. The time you put into taking complete, accurate notes will pay off as you complete the other tasks of the grievance process.

Using these notes, you can then take the next step. . . .

WRITING UP A GRIEVANCE

Some stewards are more comfortable with the spoken word than the written one. But unless your union has a policy that only chief stewards or staff representatives can write up grievances, you should try your hand at this essential part of the grievance process.

WHEN

Your contract will specify time limits for you to follow. Be aware that often the clock starts ticking from the time the incident or situation that sparked the grievance occurs. Failure to follow the time limits will usually lose the case. If you find you don't have time to investigate thoroughly, write up the grievance anyway and keep on digging. The union can always withdraw the grievance at any time.

Some contracts allow for extension of time limits by mutual consent or simply by notification. You *can* take a time extension, but it sends a message to management that the union delays. Since most managements delay, the union can put them on the defensive by not taking time limit extensions.

SIMPLICITY

A good written grievance answers three simple questions:

1. What happened, or failed to happen? (the circumstances)
2. Why is the situation a grievance? (the contention)
3. How should the employer correct the situation? (the remedy)

In most cases, each of the three questions can be answered with one sentence, so ideally the written grievance is just three sentences long. Let's take a hypothetical example.

Bill Stein says he was passed over for overtime work—four hours worth—and that the work went to a less senior employee.

To answer question 1, you would write:

"Bill Stein was unjustly passed over for overtime work on or about June 30, 1996." Make sure you use the date of the incident when you write a grievance, while still leaving room for expanding the grievance if it turns out violations occurred on other dates as well, and make sure you date the grievance on the day you submit it to management. The word *unjustly* is a good one to use in describing grievance situations.

To answer question 2, ask yourself about the action: Did it violate the contract? Did it violate past practice? Did it violate a law? In Bill's situation, you check and see that Article VIII of your contract specifies that overtime must be offered on the basis of seniority.

So you write:

"This violates Article VIII and all other relevant articles of the contract." That last phrase—"and all other relevant articles of the contract"—is a catch-all. It can be used if you later find that the action violated other sections or if you aren't sure which sections apply.

To answer question 3, ask yourself what Bill would have now if this situation had never happened. That is, what if he hadn't been passed over for the overtime? Answer: he would have gotten the overtime pay.

So you write:

"Bill Stein should be paid for four hours at the overtime pay rate and be made whole."

"Be made whole" is another catch-all that can include everything due Bill—and the union—that you may not be aware of at the time you write the grievance.

For instance, say you find supervisors are generally ignorant about assigning overtime by seniority. The union could also demand as part of the remedy that management write a memo to all supervisors instructing them on their responsibilities for assigning overtime by seniority in compliance with the contract.

Experienced stewards look at the remedy in this more strategic way—as an opportunity to gain something more from management. But that actual negotiation takes place in the grievance meeting itself, not on paper.

FLEXIBILITY IMPROVES YOUR ODDS

In order to gain the maximum advantage over management, you must take maximum advantage of the law. A written grievance should be specific enough that the employer can respond to the charge—but stated in language broad enough to argue all the relevant contract provisions and request wide avenues of relief.

A grievance should not only name the specific contract provisions that the employer has violated but also contain a qualifier that the violation is not limited to those provisions.

When you are grieving a dismissal for attendance problems, for example, you need to consider more than the usual "just cause" provision. Later you might find that management based its discharge on absences occurring during the grievant's disability leave. But if you don't cite the second contract provision, an arbitrator would probably not consider that violation.

That's why it helps to use inclusive legal language, such as: "Management has violated the collective bargaining agreement, *including, but not limited to*, Article I, Section 2.5," or "Management has violated Article 1, Section 2.5, *and all other relevant contract provisions.*"

Generally when citing dates, stewards should use the phrase *on or about*. For example, a steward might write that management allowed non–bargaining unit employees to perform bargaining unit work on December 8, 1996. During the grievance process, though, the steward might learn that the non–bargaining unit employees actually performed bargaining unit work on December 10, rather than December 8. Or, that it occurred not only on December 8, but also on November 22 and 24.

In the first situation, an arbitrator would most likely deny the union's grievance on the basis that there was no violation on December 8. In the second situation, an arbitrator would probably deny relief because of the November violations, which were not mentioned in the grievance.

To give the union a better chance of avoiding these problems at arbitration, the steward should have written the grievance as follows: "*on or about* December 8, 1996, Management allowed non–bargain-

ing unit employees to perform bargaining unit work."

Additionally, in order to get maximum possible relief, grievances should request that the grievant be "made whole in every way."

If a steward requests only that the grievant be reinstated and receive lost back pay, but not that he be "made whole," arbitrators will often refuse to award the grievant lost benefits, such as vacation time or insurance. If a steward fails to specifically request interest on back pay, some arbitrators will not include this interest in a "make whole" remedy.

A steward might, therefore, phrase a request for relief as follows: "The Union requests that the grievant be made whole in every way, including interest on back pay, for any loss resulting from Management's violation."

By using these suggestions for writing flexible grievances, stewards will protect the rights of the workers, increase the union's success rate at arbitration and maximize recovery for contract violations.

IS THERE A PRECEDENT?

One of the first things a steward does when presented with an apparent grievance is to check and see if there's a precedent—that is, if the issue has come up before in your workplace. If it has, the way it was handled and the way things were resolved should be understood and incorporated in your plan of attack.

Precedent is generally defined as "an earlier occurrence of something similar." In fact, the relationship between management and the union at a workplace is built upon a series of precedents—things done or said in bargaining and on a day-to-day basis that may serve as an example or rule to authorize or justify another such act. These precedents—sometimes written, sometimes not—pretty much govern how management and the union resolve situations.

The value in knowing and using precedents is enforcing fairness and consistency. It also means the steward isn't starting from scratch every time a problem arises. So, when you get a worker complaint, ask immediately, "Has this ever happened before?"

Start by asking the worker who makes the complaint. It's not uncommon that something might have happened before to that worker or to another worker in the same department. Sometimes workers don't tell the union when something happens to them.

Then, check with other stewards and with union representatives. Your union keeps a grievance file to track grievances and how they get resolved, as well as to use in preparing for bargaining.

By checking, you'll find out one of three things.

1 **IT'S HAPPENED BEFORE, THE UNION GRIEVED IT AND WON.** Bring this information to management's attention. That may get the problem resolved without going through the formal grievance procedure. But don't be surprised if management claims that the circumstances in this situation are "totally different"—even if they are not.

If that happens, go ahead and file a grievance. In your grievance meeting, you will highlight why the union prevailed in a previous situation. You will also show how the situations are similar and do your best to rebut management's claims that they're totally different.

2 **IT'S HAPPENED BEFORE, THE UNION GRIEVED IT AND LOST.** Look into the reason for the union's loss. It may be your turn to argue that the circumstances are different. Go ahead and file a grievance and be prepared to document the differences. If the circumstances *aren't* different you can argue that it's just a lousy precedent and your contract is silent or not effective in dealing with it.

Strategize with your union rep. Even if an earlier grievance on the subject has been lost, the union still may want to file another grievance anyway to highlight the injustice so it can play it up in the next round of bargaining. Or the union may want to undertake some other kind of action around the issue—a petition, a "button" day, some other kind of publicity, a meeting with management—to highlight the situation. Remember to keep the grievant involved and informed during this process.

Understand that precedents aren't concrete. Lousy ones should be broken, but it takes some time and some smart union action.

3 **IT'S NEVER HAPPENED BEFORE.** Conduct a thorough investigation and file a grievance if the complaint warrants it. Your good groundwork here will help the next steward who comes along and faces the same situation.

Since this is a new blast from management, discuss with other stewards and the union rep what it might mean. Maybe it's just an inept manager's screw-up. But maybe it could signal the beginning of a new management trend. Managements sometimes undertake new actions against workers to undermine the union, or because they are financially troubled, or they want to introduce technological changes or new practices, or they want to contract out.

The union's response in these situations should be carefully planned and probably will include other actions in addition to filing a grievance.

Some final advice to stewards on using precedents: Use them when it's to the union's advantage; organize like heck to break them down if they're to the union's *dis*advantage.

TEN ALL-PURPOSE STRATEGIES FOR GRIEVANCE NEGOTIATION

There are a number of generic strategies that bring results. That is, they're worth following in every grievance negotiation. Consider these ten points.

1 Have a Plan

Shooting from the hip when going into a grievance session is dangerously close to shooting yourself in the foot. Meet with your grievant beforehand. Review all the arguments. Decide on your best evidence. Talk about strategy—the plan for how the meeting is likely to go. Know what your desired outcome is.

If your grievant is going to testify, go through a rehearsal. Ask all the questions that you think management may ask when they try to undermine the grievant's testimony. Make sure the answers are what they should be.

2 No Surprises

Make sure you know everything about what happened in the case. Nothing destroys a game plan more than finding out new information in the middle of a grievance meeting, like witnesses you didn't know about or prior warnings to the grievant.

3 Don't Lose Your Cool

If you want to maintain control of the meeting, start by maintaining your self-control. That's not to say that anger or emotion cannot be effective tools for you to use. But don't be spontaneous. Any outbursts should be a part of your plan.

4 Be Realistic About Your Chances

Understand going into the session whether you're in a strong position or a weak one. What does your contract say? What about the law or enforceable policies? If the facts or precedent are clearly on your side, don't give an inch until you want to.

But most grievances aren't that black and white. Often it's a situation that is new, that wasn't anticipated the last time the contract was negotiated. Be sure you know whether you're building a case on concrete or sand. And discuss the odds in advance with your grievant.

5 Know Where the Other Side Stands

Put yourself in the employer's shoes for a minute and think about how they'll present their arguments. Consider how they will defend their actions, and know before you walk into the room what your response will be to their presentation.

6 Don't Get Personal

You want to challenge management's actions, but you don't want to attack people personally. If you make it personal, it's harder for the other side to agree that you're right.

And if management makes it personal, don't get baited into a shouting match. Don't let your grievant call the boss a stupid clown—

no matter how true it may be. It will only help prove their claim of a pattern of inappropriate conduct on the part of the grievant.

7 Ask Questions

Look for the inconsistencies in management's arguments, and pick them apart. Don't let them off the hook if they offer evasive answers. Be persistent. If their side of the story is a fairy tale, chances are there will be contradictions in their arguments, witnesses, evidence and/or statements. Find them.

8 Have Notes, Take Notes

Never go into a grievance meeting without a written outline of the arguments you're going to present, and the evidence you have to back it up.

During the meeting, take good notes —especially when management is making their case. Nothing slows supervisors down more than knowing you are writing down what they say, word for word. Good notes will also help you prepare if you need to appeal the case further.

9 Have Written Evidence

It's a fact of life—people are more likely to believe something if it's written down. It worked for the Ten Commandments; it can work for you.

If you have copies of relevant official documents, hand them out at the meeting. If your argument entails a specific chronology of events, type it up and distribute it. Written documents easily become the point of reference for everybody's discussion. If they are your documents, then you are controlling the discussion.

10 Stay United

Never disagree among yourselves during a grievance meeting. Be especially careful if management asks a question you didn't anticipate. If you need to, call for a caucus and step outside to discuss the matter in private with your grievant. Never show management that there is anything but full agreement on your side of the table.

3 PRESENTING THE GRIEVANCE

In the world of grievance presentation, as in the world of sports, the players who are prepared and who have done their homework are the most likely to win.

If you've followed the guidelines offered in Chapter 2, and done the proper investigation and research, you're well on your way. As for presenting and arguing grievances, there's no method that's guaranteed to work every time, but there are some things that work well more often than not. This chapter can help you learn to spot the potholes, the slippery steps and the bear traps in presenting your case.

IT'S SHOWTIME

If the union decides to grieve, you must prepare both yourself and the grievant for the best possible presentation.

Although any grievance procedure involves facts, personalities, strategies and timing, it helps to think in basic terms. Try to keep your eye on the ball by forming a case in your mind, and by constantly revising.

After reviewing the information for completeness and accuracy, evaluate it using the three rules of evidence:

1 Opinions vs. facts. Opinions are what people think; facts are what people see or hear. You need to weigh opinions differently than you weigh facts.

2 Facts vs. hearsay. Hearsay evidence ("John said he overheard Sally tell Nancy . . .") is not factual. Try to talk to the original source.

3 Facts must be relevant. What relates directly to the problem at hand?

WHO

Although it may seem like a strange thing to debate, some unions discourage bringing the grievant to the meeting. Others demand it, but many let the grievant and steward decide.

Taking the grievant makes strategic sense because it involves the grievant in the process and shows her exactly what happens. It gives you, the steward, an ally at the table. It shows management that workplace issues involve *real* people—not just an employee number.

Generally, the steward does all the talking in presenting the case to the supervisor. Sometimes it's effective for the grievant to participate on certain points. You should discuss and agree on these issues beforehand with the grievant.

But only bring the grievant if:

☛ you have prepared the grievant about what will happen at the meeting: what you will say, what you think *management* will say. The grievant must understand that you are conducting the meeting for the union and your lead must be followed.

☛ you have prepared some nonverbal signals with which to communicate in front of each other—passing notes, a hand on the wrist, etc. If something goes awry, you and the grievant both understand you can ask for a caucus and leave the room to regroup.

☛ it makes strategic sense for the grievant to talk about some aspect of the case. Rehearse with the grievant what she will say and when it will be said. Grievants are particularly effective because they can describe firsthand what happened and how it affected them.

☛ the grievant can emotionally handle the situation. Weigh, as best you can, the ability of the grievant to play her role without flaming out, taking a swing at someone or becoming so emotionally out of control that your case could be hurt.

WHERE

No matter what the practice has been regarding where union and management convene for grievance meetings, figure out where you will feel most comfortable and confident and ask for it.

If management won't buy your suggestion of the union hall with lots of members in the hallway, at least get a neutral area that's not a management stronghold like a management office. Or recommend taking turns on choosing locations. The choice of room won't win or lose the grievance, but it can help you and the grievant feel more comfortable.

HOW

Recognize that the grievance meeting is, in fact, a negotiation.

Determine your walk-away winning position—the best you can get *and* your bottom line—as well as what the union will settle for that's still acceptable, but doesn't undermine the contract or a member's basic rights or seriously flaw future dealings on the issue. In accepting compromises, it's not uncommon for the union or management to stipulate that the settlement is not intended to set a precedent.

Always devise fallback positions—particularly when the grievant hasn't been a total innocent and the issue is serious, like a heavy suspension or termination. You'll want to review fallback positions with the grievant, but the grievant does not have the final say on settlement. That's because the grievance is an assault on the union and its collectively bargained agreement, not just against the individual and the settlement he or she wants. If you can't get an acceptable compromise from management, the grievance should go to the next step.

Familiarity with these issues will increase your confidence and prepare you for the more weighty issues involved in grievance handling.

CHECKLIST

Once you've formed the basis of the case, then you need to think through possible pitfalls. The following checklist will help you review your strategy:

1 **Build your best case.** Decide which facts are the most convincing; keep a list so you can refer to it; show why it's in everyone's best interest to settle this now.

2 **Anticipate management.** What facts will the supervisor use? What remedies might be offered?

3 **Prepare responses.** Be ready with responses, rebuttals and compromises (regarding the remedies) that the union is willing to accept.

Your success in resolving the problem at this stage of the grievance procedure depends upon your careful preparation, your relationship with the supervisor and the strength of the union.

MANAGEMENT TACTICS IN GRIEVANCE SESSIONS

A grievance meeting should be a fair exchange between the union and management. The equity principle, long recognized by the National Labor Relations Board, points out that you are not just an employee at these meetings. As the steward, the representative of the union, you are an equal. The problem, however, is that managers often behave in ways that stack the deck against the steward.

A TYPICAL SCENARIO

Your supervisor schedules a grievance meeting for 3 p.m., just half an hour before you're due to leave work. You and the grievant meet in his office. He has you sit on low folding chairs, while he sits behind his desk. He starts talking about fishing, then spends time complaining about the economy. The phone rings. You finally get into the grievance when his secretary interrupts. Then the phone rings again. He finally gets interested in what you're saying and starts firing questions at you when the final buzzer rings to punch out.

WHAT'S REALLY GOING ON

Although this might seem to be just part of the game for the steward, it is important to understand what is going on and how it can work against you. As our scenario suggests, things to watch out for are:

☞ Your physical relationship to management.

☞ Management efforts to get you off track.

☞ Interruption.

☞ Pacing.

IT DOESN'T HAVE TO BE THIS WAY

A handy rule of thumb is to ask yourself, "Would my supervisor treat another management person this way?" If the answer is no, then you should not expect to be treated that way. Here are some hints:

1 Physical surroundings. You should not be physically dominated by the supervisor—him in a big, high chair behind a massive desk, for example, while you don't even get a place to sit and lay out your paperwork.

2 Small talk. A little chitchat is fine, but this can be used to distract you from the case at hand. Remind the supervisor what you are there for.

3 Interruptions. One interruption may be acceptable; more than that is just not necessary. Your supervisor would most likely have all calls held when meeting with another manager. He should do the same for you.

4 Pacing. Remember, this is not management's meeting only—it's just as much the union's meeting. You, too, can control the pace. If your supervisor likes to ask questions, ask him one also. If he is the quiet type, then you can be quiet too.

Grievance meeting procedures aren't written in stone, and may develop because stewards allow them to. Asserting your rights as an equal will force the supervisor to take you more seriously. It will also help you to win more grievances.

NEGOTIATING IN THE GRIEVANCE PROCESS

The real skill involved in grievance meetings—apart from preparation—is negotiating. Every steward should aim to become a shrewd negotiator—because every meeting with management about grievances is a kind of bargaining. You are trying to resolve the meaning of the contract in a particular situation as well as trying to demonstrate how management may have violated the contract. And you want the best possible

settlement for the grievant and the union.

To get the results you want from grievance negotiations, try following these guidelines.

SEPARATE THE PEOPLE FROM THE PROBLEM

Any grievance meeting has two elements—the merits of the grievance and the relationship between the parties involved. The mistake is to confuse the two.

For example, if you have a bad relationship with your supervisor, you may walk into every grievance meeting determined to show how tough you are. You become a hard negotiator, determined to win at any price. But usually such a stance triggers an equally hard response from management. Nothing gets settled—and nobody wins.

On the other hand, you don't want to be a soft negotiator. If you have a good relationship with a supervisor, you may be tempted to give in more easily to protect that relationship. But that's not good for the grievant, the union or yourself—because eventually you'll end up feeling resentful and used.

The solution is to be soft on the people and hard on the merits. It may sound psychologically difficult to be tough and friendly at the same time. But with practice, you can learn the technique. And experience has shown that it works.

Remember that you want to build and maintain a good working relationship with the supervisor. There may be times when you must agree to disagree, but you still need to keep the lines of communication open.

With individual grievances, the best approach may be to set up the grievance as a problem that you and the supervisor can work on as partners, searching for a solution that may be fair to both sides. If you have a decent relationship with your supervisor, one approach might be, for example, "Can we put our heads together to find a way to fix this?" Above all, don't let egos get in the way of a settlement that is best for the union and the grievant.

NEGOTIATE OVER INTERESTS, NOT POSITIONS

Perhaps the best way to reach such a settlement is to resist adopting a hard-and-fast position about an issue. In a negotiation, both parties start out with positions that are far from any likely settlement point. Negotiations then become a slow tug of war as each side reluctantly shifts its position closer toward settlement.

A better way is to begin by explaining your interests. For any grievance, the union's basic interest is to find a fair settlement that upholds the contract's integrity.

But management has interests, too. A supervisor is unlikely to settle any grievance in a way that adversely affects those interests. So it's up to you to find out what that supervisor needs.

When you know what management's interests are, you can focus your efforts on the next step—a search for workable solutions that meet the interests of both sides.

INVENT OPTIONS FOR MUTUAL GAIN

Mutual gains are often possible in negotiations because both parties share some interests. Inventing options can help you satisfy the other side's interests as well as your own.

Assume that both sides can achieve something positive in each grievance negotiation—even if it is just an understanding or an improved relationship. At a minimum, bringing multiple options into a grievance meeting can provide some new energy and a different focus for discussion.

With experience, stewards can learn how and when to practice these guidelines most effectively. In all cases, the goal of these suggested strategies remains the same as for any negotiation: to win settlements that are consistent with the contract and add strength to the union.

UNWELCOME SURPRISES

No matter how well you've prepared a case, there will come a time when the unexpected happens. Here are some examples, and how you can deal with them.

THE GRIEVANT'S STORY CHANGES

You're sitting in a grievance meeting with a grievant whose story you have reviewed countless times. But in the middle of the meeting the grievant tells another part of the story that you have *never* heard, and it changes the nature of the situation entirely.

Try not to look surprised—and ask for a caucus. It's all you can do.

Use the caucus to figure out how this new piece of information fits into the case. Apply your own "unjust" test: if what happened to the grievant still seems unjust, you may have to concede the new information to management as a minor point, but argue that overall, other facts are more important and contribute to the "unjustness" of the situation.

If you can't figure out a new strategy, ask for a postponement of the meeting. If the new information is too damaging, the union may have to drop the grievance. At a minimum, though, try to buy your side some time to regroup and consult with the chief steward or union representative.

Thorough preparation with the grievant and checking out the situation with a variety of people can help prevent this, but even the most experienced stewards report this happens to them periodically.

NEW EVIDENCE POPS UP

Then there's the memo or letter that you didn't know existed, and management whips it out at the grievance meeting.

If you made an information request from management before the meeting and did not receive that particular item, that's an unfair labor practice under the National Labor Relations Act and usually under other labor legislation as well.

If you didn't request information, your strategy will depend on the nature of the "paper." If it's something other than a piece of correspondence to the grievant—a memo to the personnel files, for example, or a memo from one supervisor to another—minimize the contents of the communication by emphasizing that management did not make the grievant or the union aware of the issue.

If the "paper" is a disciplinary memo or letter to the grievant, you're in a pickle if you are claiming that the grievant was not aware of a discipline. If the discipline was unjust for other reasons, focus on arguing those reasons as more important than the "awareness" issue.

WHAT POLICY CHANGE?

The union leadership should keep stewards informed of new policies that result both from collective bargaining and from the normal labor-management exchanges that occur over the term of the contract.

But sometimes there's a breakdown and a steward will find out about it when it's too late—like at a grievance meeting.

When you're caught with egg on your face, your touchstone again is your judgment on the unjustness of the situation. If it still seems unjust, is there something else you can hang it on—another policy, past practice or some other section of the contract? Your "quick recovery" line here is: "Despite that new policy, the action against the grievant is still unjust."

If you come up short, make sure your union leadership knows the issue needs to be addressed in the next labor-management committee meeting or next round of bargaining.

MINIMIZING SURPRISE

In addition to thorough preparation (including asking the grievant point blank right before you go into the meeting, "Is there anything else I should know before we go into this room?"), requesting information from the employer and keeping abreast of new practices and policies, you can also minimize the impact of surprises by maintaining a credible reputation with management. If you have a reputation for being well prepared, an occasional "surprise" won't totally devastate it. Nor will it be irreparably hurt if you have a strong, united workforce behind you.

Besides—don't you have some surprises to spring on management along the way?

ARBITRATION: THE END OF THE LINE

In most collective bargaining agreements the final step in the grievance process is arbitration. When labor and management can't work out the problem through use of the grievance machinery, it's agreed that they will submit the dispute to an impartial outsider—an arbitrator.

There are a number of positive things about being able to take unresolved disputes to arbitration, and a number of negatives as well. First, the good things.

THE UP SIDE

For starters, the decision as to what rights the union has under its contract is made by a neutral third party. Unlike the steps of the grievance procedure, in which a series of closed-minded management representatives can just say no, an arbitration results in a decision being issued by someone who isn't connected financially or organizationally to either side.

Second, private sector arbitration awards, and most public sector awards as well, are final and binding. For all practical purposes, there's usually no appeal of an arbitration award.

Third, resolving a dispute through arbitration is almost always quicker, easier and less expensive than taking a case to court.

Finally, after a hard-fought legal battle, a formal outside finding that the employer has violated your contract rights packs a punch that a grievance settlement lacks.

But it's important to recognize the limitations of arbitrating cases, as well.

THE DOWN SIDE

There's no need to quarrel with the fact that it's better to win an arbitration than to lose one. But just the same, the focus of a steward's efforts should be on resolving disputes at the lowest level, in the shortest time possible. Except for a rare situation where tactical considerations come into play, it's a mistake to hold back when you argue a grievance, thinking you'd rather win the Big One at arbitration. In the eyes of your members, the faster you can deliver the goods, the better their union looks to them. Justice delayed is justice denied.

And keep in mind that you've got a responsibility as steward to use the union's resources carefully. While an arbitration may be cheaper than litigating a court case, it's *incredibly* more expensive than settling the dispute at the grievance level.

Remember that when a case goes to arbitration, you—and the union—lose control in a number of ways. The grievance steps are close to the workplace, where members are near the action. You and they have ready access to the facts it makes sense to present, and you've got a shop-floor understanding of the big picture—things like how winning with the wrong argument in this case might set a precedent that makes things worse for future cases.

An arbitration award can also be a big surprise—for both sides. When you settle a grievance, it's on terms the union and the employer understand and find acceptable. Sometimes an arbitrator looking for a way to cut the baby in half will issue an award that doesn't really give *either* side what they want. Worse yet, an arbitrator who doesn't understand the day-to-day realities of your workplace can make an award that leaves both sides scratching their heads, with the issue that triggered the grievance still unresolved.

GRIEVANCES THAT WIN AT ARBITRATION

It's important to anticipate that some grievances *will* go to arbitration, and to take the necessary steps to maximize your percentage of wins. Let's look at each part of the grievance process to see how to build a winner.

FILING

Including too much or too little when you write up a grievance can come back to haunt you. If you specify certain articles and sections of the contract as having been violated, that can give the employer a foot in the door to argue to an arbitrator that *other* contract violations the union is claiming are after-the-fact and shouldn't be taken seriously. And if you stake out a lot more ground than you actually can cover when putting forth your evidence at arbitration, it can make your entire case start to look shaky.

Tip

Write up your grievance to include enough specifics to be taken seriously, but don't box yourself in; use phrases mentioned earlier such as "including, but not necessarily limited to, the following provisions of the contract." And after you set forth whatever specific relief you are requesting in the grievance, always add "and any other appropriate relief."

DISCOVERY

Once you're at the stage of preparing for an arbitration hearing, the union has rights—usually under both contract and law—to conduct discovery. That means getting documents and other information from management that relate to the issues in the case. But human nature being what it is (and some crafty lawyers being who they are), it may be that by the time you're scheduled for arbitration it's too late to uncover some of the really juicy stuff. Your employer's labor relations experts have already swept quite a bit under the rug.

Tip

Poke around for as much information as you can early on in the grievance process, perhaps by getting explanations from talkative supervisors about what's really going on, or asking for copies of paperwork. Use the rights you have to obtain information needed to evaluate and pursue a grievance, so that you can get the goods before they're gone.

ARGUING

Either side can make things worse at arbitration by being too talkative or too closed-mouthed during grievance meetings. On the one hand, there's no point in holding back when you might well have enough evidence to make the employer back down. On

---

Tip

Never, ever, stop employer representatives from talking during a grievance investigation or meeting. Many a grievance is won when Dr. Arbitrator diagnoses a case of foot-in-mouth disease: when what a supervisor said at last month's grievance meeting doesn't square with what the employer's lawyer is arguing at this month's arbitration. The flip side of that coin is to make sure that you and the grievant don't give management information that'll come back to haunt you; don't volunteer too much information.

Also, write it down! A dispute about what a management representative said at the time the grievance was processed may be heard at an arbitration many months away; notes you took *at the time* will be valuable.

---

the other hand, if it doesn't look likely that a case can be resolved, why let the boss know what you have now; better to let management witnesses be surprised by the smoking gun on the witness stand at arbitration, rather than giving advance warning and the time to think up a convincing story. Lots of times, knowing which cards to play and which to hold on to boils down to making a difficult judgment call, and then hoping for the best.

So when thinking about the smartest way to approach grievance processing, remember that just as with many things in life, sometimes you'll be successful by starting at the end and then working your way to the beginning.

MAKING A LOSING GRIEVANCE INTO A WINNER

It hurts when all your efforts to win a grievance fail. Even if you've won the last half dozen grievances you've presented, the sting of a loss can have a devastating impact on your co-workers. Swift action, though, can minimize the damage and sometimes even create an opportunity for something positive.

First, do damage control. Many stewards have a tendency to want to hide the losers, but rumors are going to spread anyway and it is best for the grievant and everyone else to hear it straight from you. Meet face to face with the grievant and take the time necessary to explain the situation. This may be one of the most difficult things you are called upon to do as a steward, but in the long run it will do much more for your reputation for integrity to honestly tell the story. In some cases this will be all you can do, but at least you have told the truth and you can move on from there.

In many cases, though, you can do a lot more. Lost grievances are often justice gone awry. They often underscore the unreasonableness of your employer, or the fact that arbitration is far from a perfect process. Most of all, lost grievances point out the importance of going beyond the traditional grievance procedure and using the power of the membership to pressure the employer to live up to both the agreement and past practice.

STEVE MAGNUSON

USE THE LOSS TO EDUCATE

Don't whine about the loss; use it to teach something new to your membership. If it was a case of management denying the most senior person a job because a junior person was judged to have better qualifications, review this section of the contract with your members. Is the language strong enough? What has the past practice been? Was it a case of not enough evidence or witnesses to bolster your case? Use this as an opportunity to review the importance of grievance investigation, getting everything in writing and carefully preparing any witnesses.

Grievances often are lost at arbitration, a process many workers do not fully understand. This is an excellent time to discuss the arbitration process.

CONSIDER ALTERNATIVE STRATEGIES

A gray area of your contract or a poor arbitrator's decision can end up making your employer look petty, evil or worse. Rather than just complaining about the system, publicize it, have fun with it, and mobilize your members to force change. This can include button or T-shirt days, petitions and other tactics designed to show union solidarity and let the employer know that you are still not satisfied. It can also include informational picketing, working to rule and other strategies to pressure the employer to correct the problem. Remember to start with small, low-risk actions to build commitment before trying more elaborate schemes. Also, beyond very small departmental actions, you also need to coordinate any activity with other stewards and the local union leadership. Whatever tactic you use, showing management unity and solidarity after a loss is very important and will do much to minimize the temporary setback.

LOOKING AT THE BIG PICTURE

Many stewards don't realize that you can achieve your objective even when filing a losing grievance. Consider the following.

SHINE A LIGHT

Nothing is more frustrating to a union advocate than to hear from management, "That's just you complaining; none of the people you say you represent care." Sometimes a grievance—or two or three or more—is necessary to get management to acknowledge that a particular problem is real, and needs to be addressed.

FIRE A WARNING SHOT

There are times when it wouldn't make sense to fight management to the death on a particular action—a price increase in the employer's cafeteria, for example. By itself it may not be serious enough to take a case to arbitration, or it may be that the members just aren't riled up enough about it. But it might make a great deal of sense to have a mass grievance filing, putting management on notice that their action has not gone unnoticed, and that if they try the same maneuver again, they may well have a serious fight on their hands.

FORGE EMPLOYEE UNITY

It may well be that there is no immediate practical resolution of a particular problem. But a grievance—particularly a group grievance—might be just what's needed to start building solidarity among those wronged by a particular supervisor or policy. If employees get it together enough to take a small action, like filing a grievance, maybe soon they'll be ready to do whatever it takes to fight—and win—on this or a bigger issue.

It's true that enforcing the provisions of a collective bargaining agreement is the most common reason for filing a grievance. But we need to keep in mind that there are other valid reasons for grieving, limited only by our own creativity.

4 HANDLING THE MOST COMMON TYPES OF GRIEVANCES

Nearly everyone who brings you a grievance is sure that their problem is unique. It is, but only because it's unique to *them*. It's a good bet that something very much like it has happened before, and probably many times.

That's why it's a good idea to get acquainted with the most common types of grievances. In this chapter, we look at the various kinds of grievances and disputes and provide guidelines for handling them. Most grievances will fall into one or more of these categories.

ABSENTEEISM AND TARDINESS DISCIPLINES

Almost all stewards have to deal with absenteeism and tardiness. The following principles, drawn from arbitration decisions, are intended to give some rules of the road for handling these all-too-common problems.

There has been a trend over the last few years toward instituting no-fault attendance programs. Such programs automatically assign points or demerits for absences or tardiness, with or without advance notice, regardless of the reason for the occurrence. While most arbitrators uphold

these programs when unions challenge them, this does not mean that there cannot be exceptions—especially when the absence is beyond the worker's control, such as in cases of sudden illness or a family tragedy.

Can management unilaterally begin a new absenteeism program? Most arbitrators say yes, although they also require employers to notify workers of the program's implications and what will happen if the rules are violated. The union can insist that the program be discussed before it's instituted, but it cannot stop the employer from establishing a reasonable set of rules covering absenteeism and tardiness.

What must an employer do to properly enforce its rules? The list is specific:

☞ Conduct a thorough investigation before an employee is disciplined for absenteeism.

☞ Make an attempt to deal with underlying problems causing absences or tardiness.

☞ Follow a progressive discipline policy—that is, verbal warning, written warning, suspension(s), and only after all that, termination.

☞ Counsel the worker. Following counseling, the employee can be disciplined only if it's clear he can't be expected to resume work and maintain acceptable attendance levels.

☞ Prove a clear pattern of behavior exists that has an adverse effect on the employer's ability to conduct business. (Even chronic illness can be grounds for discharge if the employer's operation is adversely affected.)

What can a steward do to protect workers? Here are some approaches:

☞ Make sure that management has documented its case. It is not uncommon for a manager to screw up and lump insubordination with absenteeism, which usually involves different rules and should be treated separately.

☞ Try to get help for the worker. If the worker has a drinking or drug problem, family troubles, or a health problem, make sure that he gets the assistance needed to deal with the underlying issues before he gets fired on top of other obstacles he faces.

☞ Protect older, long-service workers. Employees with good records and high seniority are hurt more by termination than younger people, and the union should do what it can to protect them both before and after they have been disciplined.

☞ Make sure that all employees are treated the same when it comes to absenteeism or tardiness. Treatment should be consistent.

☞ Sometimes workers are put in a situation where their absence is beyond their control, or they may not have been able to notify management for some reason. It may be a health problem, problems with their automobile, or something else.

☞ If the employee's absence did not work a hardship on the employer, be sure to raise that in the grievance procedure.

☞ There normally is a system for washing out old absences from the personal record, and the steward must be sure that the employer is not raising old incidents that should no longer be considered. Check any time limits.

☞ Make sure that the employer representative did a thorough investigation before disciplining the worker. Failure to do so is one of the reasons that arbitrators frequently cite when they reinstate discharged workers.

☞ Check the agreement and the absenteeism policies to make sure management didn't violate its own rules or the contract.

☞ If the absenteeism was of a minor nature, then make sure management doesn't try to discharge someone who ought just to be written up or receive a short suspension instead. Be sure the punishment isn't worse than the crime. And, make sure they counted right when adding up the occurrences of absence or tardiness.

Don't forget to check your labor agreement and the employer's rules as part of your preliminary investigation!

WORK PERFORMANCE

Work performance issues are one of the most common sources of labor-management conflict. While specific contract language is very important in determining worker rights in these cases, there are some solid guidelines and considerations for stewards to weigh. Here are some basics to look at when faced with grievances revolving around work performance.

EMPLOYEE NEGLIGENCE

If a worker doesn't carry out his duties in a diligent and careful manner, and negligence causes damage to employer property, arbitrators are inclined to uphold disciplinary actions, especially if they don't involve discharge. Malicious or intentional misbehavior may result in a discharge being upheld, even for the first incident.

INCOMPETENCE

It's tougher to discipline someone for incompetence when other methods of dealing with the problem may be more appropriate. If there are alternatives, such as giving the employee an easier job, retraining or otherwise helping the worker to come up to expected performance, the supervisor should try them first. If the problem is of long standing, there is always a question as to why an allegedly incompetent person wasn't disciplined earlier.

MEETING PRODUCTION STANDARDS

Management has a right to set reasonable standards and to enforce them through discipline. Production standards may be set in several ways—time study, past experience, production records, even rule of thumb. Generally, there is contract language governing production standards, and the union can challenge the legitimacy of the standard in the grievance procedure. The employee is entitled to due process: prior warning, written warning, suspension and discharge only as a final step. An employee's production record is key to supporting disciplinary action for not meeting production standards.

PROGRESSIVE DISCIPLINE APPLIED

Did the employer notify the employee and apply progressive discipline? In one case, a sanitary cleaner with twenty-five years of service had his discharge upheld because he was warned in writing six times about his deteriorating work. The union and the employer had agreed to give him three months to improve, and the union could not show that improvement had occurred.

SERIOUSNESS RULE

Did the discipline imposed fit the seriousness of the problem? If a work performance problem is a minor one, the imposed penalty should be minor: the penalty should fit the "crime."

LENGTH OF TIME

How long has the problem existed? If management has put up with poor performance for many years, it must demonstrate that something has changed before it can invoke major disciplinary action. Management must show a stepped-up level of enforcement of standards for everyone as well as a serious attempt to work with the employee in question before invoking discipline.

EMPLOYEE'S HISTORY

What is the production and discipline history? It is necessary to review the worker's production record, identify previous disciplines and develop a clear understanding of the problem. Make sure the worker knew what the production standard called for; determine whether other employees could make the standard; and establish how far below expected production levels the worker was. Try to determine whether health or other personal problems were affecting production.

LENGTH OF SERVICE

How long has the employee been working there? Long-service workers face extra problems: their ability to find another job is impaired if they are over forty years of age. Arbitrators are reluctant to uphold discharge of long-service employees, since there is always an implication that action should have been taken earlier. They generally find that other means of improving production should have been tried.

EACH CASE IS DIFFERENT

The arbitration record shows that few employees are fired for poor work performance, generally because wide variations in ability or interest in doing a good job are tolerated by employers. It is far more likely that employees will be punished for absenteeism or tardiness. Where workloads are clear and standards are consistently enforced, employees are more likely to be successfully disciplined. Counseling and retraining are far better methods for dealing with work performance problems.

APPRAISAL SYSTEMS USED

Nobody likes to be put under a microscope and examined, but that's what happens to millions of workers across the country every day as employers undertake performance appraisals.

Most unionists are unaware just how shockingly unscientific even the most sophisticated of appraisal systems really are. While there are some governmental guidelines on the hiring of new employees, there are no regulations on how performance appraisals must be handled.

Performance appraisal often goes on constantly, sometimes formalized and sometimes not, and it has a big effect on the workers on which it is used.

These are some of the performance appraisal systems being used by employers today, and some of the concerns trade unionists have about them:

Electronic Monitoring

It's increasingly common for employee telephone conversations or electronic mail to be monitored, or for workers' actions to be monitored by video cameras. Speed and flow of keyboard or other computer-linked work can be monitored as well. Things are getting so bad, according to a 1993 *Macworld* magazine report, that 20 million workers are subjected to electronic eavesdropping. These invasions of privacy may or may not be related to performance of other jobs in an organization, and may not fairly portray overall performance.

Merit-Rating

These appraisal systems, which can take a variety of forms, may be bought off-the-shelf or developed in-house. They may or may not be job-related, and very often get into employee characteristics having nothing to do with the job in question. The merit-rating systems take two major forms:

☛ *Quantitative.* Usually a checklist is used, and worker performance is assessed along some kind of continuum. Weight is given to different kinds of performance. A point score is derived, and this score is ranked against some composite scoring system ranging from ideal to failing. There may be a problem of job-relatedness, validity (is management measuring characteristics that really affect job performance?) and reliability (are results consistent from one application to another?) with this method.

☞ *Free-written rating.* Someone supposedly familiar with the employee submits a written report. The report then becomes the basis for a wide variety of future personnel decisions. Problems with this method center around the skills and biases of the person doing the rating, job-relatedness, validity and reliability.

Productivity

Actual employee productivity measures are recorded, and job decisions are heavily affected by that one factor. It usually is quite job-related, but may be influenced by factors not within the employee's control.

Peer Reviews

Fellow employees' impressions about the person are collected, collated and summarized. The problems here may be bias, job-relatedness and reliability.

Self-Appraisals

Here the employee is presumed to be the best judge of his own performance. There may be problems of bias, disagreement with others' ratings and predictability of future performance.

Quality

Employee error or reject rates may be collected and used to assess performance. There may be problems of attributing quality problems to the proper person, job-relatedness and reliability.

Critical Incidents

It's not uncommon for so-called critical incidents to be used as part of the performance appraisal system, in which certain situations are used to assess the past or future performance of workers. The problems here are consistency of treatment, job-relatedness, validity and reliability.

Interpersonal Relations

These measures include such items as whether the employee gets along well with others, whether he has a good attitude toward fellow employees, helps other employees, responds to instructions enthusiastically, and in general gives evidence of friendliness and warmth toward others. While these characteristics may be important, measuring them is fraught with risk of bias, problems of reliability and validity, and not least, job-relatedness.

Absence or Tardiness

An employee may be assessed on concrete measures such as absence rate, number of times tardy, taking long lunch hours or too long breaks, all of which might affect productivity and performance. While these are legitimate concerns and easy to measure, care must be taken to assure that all people are assessed uniformly and that the standards applied are not unrealistically rigorous.

What should a steward look for when examining appraisal systems? First, the union should formally request the employer to inform the union which appraisal systems are in place, how often they're applied and what use is made of the results (wage increases, promotions, discipline, retraining, counseling or whatever). Then, try to secure a copy of the system, so you can have someone take a look at it to determine whether it is job-related, reliable, valid, consistent in application from one person to another, and free of bias—a major problem.

If you think that the appraisal method in use ought to be discussed, talk to your union officers and let them know about your concerns. Keep in mind that since performance reviews may have an impact on wages, hours and conditions, the union has a right to discuss them with the employer.

FIGHTING BAD APPRAISALS

If a worker's tangible benefits are adversely affected by a performance appraisal, he has the right to file a grievance under *most* labor agreements. The employee usually has a right to ask a steward to be present during disciplinary meetings, so make sure your co-workers know that.

BEFORE MEETING WITH MANAGEMENT

Find out whether management used a standard performance appraisal form. If so, what were the employee's ratings? Make sure that the rating factors are *job-related*. Check with other workers to confirm that what management said about the worker is really the case—or isn't. Whichever way it goes, make sure you get specific information so you can be comfortable in either telling the worker the union can't fight the evaluation or that you are armed with evidence to fight the case before management.

If your investigation reveals that the employee does have serious performance problems, give him a chance to explain things, and then make your decision. If you decide the employee was unfairly treated, then let him know and say that the union is willing to pursue the case.

Before sitting down with management, be sure you and the worker agree on the facts, and that in fact he wants your support and involvement.

b.

a.

- ☛ Was the employee in question *counseled* before action was taken?

- ☛ Was the appraisal valid? Were the questions asked in the review form *job-related?* If management is measuring leadership, make sure there is need for it in the job held by the employee.

- ☛ Is there evidence of bias? If the manager or supervisor demonstrates prejudice or bias toward the employee, nail down the fact that this person is being treated differently from others you represent.

- ☛ Is this a bad attitude report? This is a classic excuse for taking action against an employee without having to explain. The employer claims that the aggrieved is argumentative, obstinate or fails to demonstrate proper respect to management or others. Make sure that management proves that the employee's behavior is in fact as they say, and if so, that it adversely affected the employer in some way.

If incompetence is charged, it's a difficult accusation for management to sustain—especially for employees who have been on the job for many years. You have to assess the performance of the aggrieved against that of others in the department

AT THE MEETING

Meet with management and go over the facts as you know them. Questions that should be answered include:

before accepting management's finding. Bear in mind the worker's years of prior service.

Remember that it violates federal law to discriminate against workers because of their union activities, or older workers simply because of their age—no matter what excuses are used, like "attitude" or "lack of cooperation" or something else too vague to document. Older workers may be downgraded on their performance reviews simply because the employer wants to get rid of them.

In handling performance review cases—barring real evidence to the contrary—be sure you give the benefit of the doubt to workers who come to you with the complaint that their evaluation doesn't reflect the real quality of their work.

RULE VIOLATIONS

Most every steward has to deal with grievances arising from alleged violations of the employer's rules. While no one questions an employer's right to unilaterally establish reasonable workplace rules not inconsistent with law or your union contract, the right is not an absolute one and the way the rules are applied can be challenged by the union.

In general, a contract's management rights clause spells out the employer's right to establish rules. The key question is whether a given rule is reasonable and just. Most arbitrators agree that the mere existence of what appears to be an unfair rule is not a grievable issue. Rather, the time to challenge a rule is after it is applied in a way that does harm to a group or individual.

How do stewards deal with such rule violation cases? Here are some principles to be aware of that can help a worker who is victimized by an unfair or stupid rule.

IS THE RULE APPLIED WITH AN EVEN HAND TO ALL PERSONS COVERED BY IT?

Sometimes rules are enforced more vigorously with women than with men, with unskilled workers than with skilled workers, or when help is hard to get as compared to periods when unemployment is high. Or, one person may be fired for a rule violation while another has merely been suspended for the same thing.

WERE THERE EXTENUATING CIRCUMSTANCES AT THE TIME THE INCIDENT OCCURRED?

Even when a steward might agree the worker violated a legitimate rule, should the employee's age, past record, years of service or family problems be taken into account to reduce the penalty?

WERE WORKERS NOTIFIED WHEN THE RULE WAS ESTABLISHED, CHANGED OR PUT BACK IN FORCE?

Did the employer make a special effort to let susceptible workers know about the rule? Did the employer notify affected persons concerning penalties that might be imposed? Can the employer produce a record documenting that employees were contacted?

WAS THE RULE UNDERSTANDABLE?

The employer is obliged to make the rule absolutely clear—exactly what behavior is unacceptable, and exactly what penalty will be imposed. Thus, if "extended absence" may meet with discipline, just exactly how long is "extended"? How many hours, days or weeks? Also, different rules might be cited in the same incident, and the different rules may call for different penalties. It has to be clear which rule applies to the case in question, and why.

DOES THE RULE CAUSE AN UNDUE HARDSHIP ON SOME OF THE WORKERS IT COVERS?

Let's say a rule allows workers a ten-minute break every morning. You could argue that workers who are far removed from the rest room or coffee machine can't really use the break period as effectively as those working close to the toilet or break room.

DID MANAGEMENT DISCUSS THE RULE OR CONSULT WITH THE UNION PRIOR TO ESTABLISHING OR CHANGING THE RULE?

The union is entitled to notification and/or an opportunity to discuss changes in working conditions resulting from the application of the rule.

WAS DUE PROCESS FOLLOWED?

Most contracts call for verbal warnings first, followed by written warnings, then suspension and finally discharge if nothing else works. And, increasingly, employers are considered to be responsible for counseling wayward employees or offering retraining assistance if they have a work performance problem.

WAS MANAGEMENT ABLE TO PROVE THAT AN EMPLOYEE WAS GUILTY OF A RULE VIOLATION?

Circumstantial or hearsay evidence is weak and must be considered as such. It could also implicate someone else, not just the accused person.

DOES THE RULE SERVE A PRACTICAL PURPOSE TO THE EMPLOYER?

If violation of the rule harms neither the employer nor employees, then why does it exist at all?

PAST PRACTICES

Usually, a steward files a grievance after management violates the union contract. But at times the issue concerns a past practice that isn't covered in the contract. Can you still win? The answer may well be yes.

Arbitrators recognize that not all agreements get reduced to writing, and not all benefits are formalized in a written contract. So it's important to give careful consideration to worker complaints that don't appear to have support in the agreement.

This could involve anything: changing the way paychecks are distributed, perhaps, or altering the way people are called in to work. In other words, a basic issue that can be resolved by a verbal agreement. This is what the term "custom and practice" arises from—past practice. Here are the principles to keep in mind when trying to determine whether something is a past practice.

THE CUSTOM OR PRACTICE MUST BE CERTAIN AND UNEQUIVOCAL

The steward must be able to show that the past practice is clear and straightforward. The practice should be easy to understand and be used widely throughout the workplace.

THE PAST PRACTICE MUST BE CLEARLY STATED AND MUST HAVE BEEN ACTED UPON

It helps if you can show that the practice was jointly determined. If the employer can demonstrate that the practice was unilaterally instituted by management without union input, then the steward is in a weaker position.

If the steward can prove that management was aware of the custom and made no attempt to eliminate it, you are on firmer ground. Arbitrators have held that employers, instead of changing a practice during the life of an agreement, should serve notice that they will propose to get rid of it when the contract expires. If the practice causes no inconvenience or extra cost to the employer, that's even better for the union.

THE PRACTICE MUST BE FIXED, ESTABLISHED AND ABLE TO BE PROVEN TO EXIST OVER A REASONABLE PERIOD OF TIME

It helps if you can show that there have been multiple grievances filed previously and settled, even if the settlement was in the first step and there is no written record.

If the underlying reason for the past practice is eliminated, then the employer can cancel it.

The idea here is that management has a right to make changes—for example, removing sandwich or coffee machines if the need for them is eliminated by the creation of a cafeteria. And remember that an employer has a general right to change work methods, equipment and the work process as part of managing the enterprise.

THE PRACTICE MUST NOT CONFLICT WITH LAWS OR STATUTES

Don't expect an arbitrator to support you if the practice violates the law, such as the unauthorized filling of an employee's gas tank with the employer's fuel. Likewise, if the custom encourages unsafe or dangerous working conditions, then it's not likely to be supported by an arbitrator.

A CONTRACT MAY PROTECT PAST PRACTICES

Sometimes a contract includes a clause stating that specific past practices will be continued during the life of the agreement. This obviously protects those past practices, but the language may also be interpreted to mean that other *unstated* practices are continued as well. It helps to link a past practice with the contract, even if it's just the general clause that includes bargaining over wages, hours and working conditions.

THE PRACTICE PROVIDES SOMETHING OF BENEFIT TO EMPLOYEES

First and foremost, if the practice gives employees some benefit and is well established by precedent, then it is more likely that the arbitrator will support its continuance.

INSUBORDINATION

Cases involving suspension or discharge for refusal to follow instructions—insubordination—can be especially difficult. However, enough have been brought to arbitration that previous decisions provide some guidelines for how to best deal with this problem.

☛ If the worker appears to have been singled out for special punishment for refusing to follow orders, your grounds for pursuing a grievance will be strengthened. If normal workplace practices have permitted similar behavior previously, call that to the attention of management. One superior may tolerate a greater degree of so-called insubordination than another.

☛ You'll want to determine if the insubordination occurred during an unusually tense situation. Sometimes a specific event aggravates the relationship between worker and management: a deadline that is putting heavy pressure on the supervisor, for example, or a serious family problem affecting the worker.

☛ Check your contract: does it protect an employee's refusal to obey? For example, the contract may allow the worker to have a steward present during discussions about behavior, but the supervisor didn't permit it in the case at hand.

☛ Was guilt clearly established? Did the employer furnish witnesses or produce confirming evidence that the insubordination actually occurred? If multiple acts of insubordination are claimed, make sure that the *entire* work record is reviewed.

☛ Was the employee *set up* to be insubordinate *after* the decision was made to discipline him? It is one thing to warn an employee of impending suspension or discharge, and quite another to provoke the employee into refusing to obey an order in front of a witness.

☛ If the refusal was prompted by a belief that there was risk of danger to the worker or someone else, then discipline may not be upheld in arbitration. However, if the employee knew about the risk ahead of time, then she had an obligation to report it to the proper person immediately.

☛ Management must make orders clear and understandable. If, for example, an instruction was issued in a way it could not be properly heard, the discipline may have been unfair.

- Orders should not be of such a nature as to be an affront, indignity or invasion of personal privacy. However, arbitrators will uphold body or locker searches when there is evidence of dishonesty, or drug and alcohol tests where such tests have been agreed to or are of long standing, or where the employer's operation may be affected by improper behavior. Public concern about use of drugs on the job has resulted in arbitrators looking at the issue as serious, so requirements to submit to such tests are more and more common.

- As a general rule, if repeated failure of a worker to follow instructions causes harm to others, or interrupts production of goods and services basic to the employer's operation, the discipline is likely to be upheld. Still, the employer must follow due process and regular, agreed-upon steps when disciplining.

- Even when there's no question the worker screwed up, a steward will still want to consider whether the punishment was excessive. The union will want to urge that a worker's previous years of loyal, effective service be taken into account. Is the employer inconsistent in applying standards of behavior? Asking for lighter punishment in specific cases is the standard system for handling borderline cases involving good employees.

The best advice a steward can give his members is to check with the union before refusing to obey a direct order, or else obey the order and file an immediate grievance. The fundamental assumption, of course, is that the order or instruction is related to operation of the organization and not the personal needs of a manager. When in doubt, always go back to find out how the union has handled similar cases in the past.

PROMOTIONS

Promotion grievances are tough. If you win, the grievant is happy but the person *losing* the promotion can be mad as hell. If you *lose* the grievance, the grievant can be mad as hell but the person scoring the new job is happy. When both parties are in the bargaining unit, you're in as close to a no-win situation as you can get. Still, the terms of the contract have to be enforced. It's all part of the job of keeping the union strong and making sure the contract is honored by your employer. Promotion grievances may not be any fun, but looking out for the following benchmarks may make handling them a little easier.

DISCRIMINATION

It's always wise to check into whether there were overtones of race or sex discrimination in granting the promotion, or if evidence of favoritism exists in the employer's determination of who got the job. Arbitrators are sensitive to changes in laws regarding equal employment opportunities without regard to race, sex, national origin, religion, age and, most recently, disability. Arbitrators tend to favor the underdog where discrimination can be shown to exist.

THE BASIS OF DETERMINING ABILITY

When looking at whether a worker has the ability to do a job, remember that ability has to relate specifically to job performance. If there is testing of a worker, the test must be appropriate: the United States Supreme Court has ruled that employer-required tests must be *job-related*. For many years, employers used standardized psychological and aptitude tests originally developed for estimating students' scholastic ability. Now employers must limit their use of tests to those that are closely related to the job being filled. Many employers still use tests that contain sections and questions that have nothing to do with the job in question. Look at the test: does it really measure the qualities needed in particular jobs?

Also be aware that if a promotion is denied on the basis of past performance or so-called merit reviews, you have the right (with the permission of the grieving employee) to ask to see that information. If the employer refuses, citing confidentiality, you can ask that it be reviewed by a neutral third party, such as a minister or respected community leader.

THE LABOR AGREEMENT

If your contract stipulates that seniority determines promotion, then seniority, not ability, should be the determining factor. If the agreement states that promotions are on the basis of seniority *and* ability, then the senior applicant must appear to possess sufficient ability to perform the job. If the contract says "where ability is approximately equal, then seniority prevails," then you must judge whether the successful candidate was head and shoulders above the senior person who was denied the job.

None of these judgments are easy to prove except the first, seniority. Sometimes the agreement sets forth more than two factors—past performance or attendance, perhaps—in addition to seniority and ability.

In those cases, the steward must investigate management's evaluation of the additional factors to check whether its decision was appropriate in terms of the workers' employment history.

THE JOB POSTING OR JOB DESCRIPTION

The steward must understand the nature of the job being filled. Is it a new job, or one recently changed? If so, do the qualifications appear reasonable or appropriate? Are the qualifications related to the *major duties* involved in the position? Do the duties that are being made the basis for denying someone the job really exist? Are the duties something that are absolutely essential to the job, and is it necessary that the person have prior qualifications? If there is a job evaluation system, see what the job write-up has to say about effort, skill and responsibility requirements and whether they conform to the qualifications stated.

CURRENT OR PREVIOUS JOB HOLDERS

Check this out as well: If current or previous job holders had qualifications that were clearly higher, did they have those qualifications *prior* to being hired or promoted into the job . . . or were they given an opportunity to learn them *on* the job? Additionally, if there is a job evaluation sys-

tem, do the evaluations on the skill or responsibility factors support what management is now claiming to be entry qualifications?

PAST INDISCRETIONS

Try to assess the prior record of the unsuccessful applicant to see if management is inappropriately holding some past sin against her, and using denial of promotion as a form of punishment. Withholding job opportunities because of past problems is out of bounds as punishment unless permitted by accepted rules or the contract, or the previous pattern of behavior would clearly have an adverse effect on performance of the job in question.

EACH CASE MUST BE DEALT WITH ON ITS MERITS

While the preceding principles provide standard questions that must be raised, stewards still need to review the contract language governing promotions, check the actual facts of the case and remember to determine whether the qualifications being used to select workers are appropriate.

OFF-DUTY CONDUCT

What you do on your own time and away from work is none of your employer's business, right? The answer to that question may surprise you.

Sure, unions realize that arbitrators constantly uphold management's right to discipline employees for just cause when the misconduct takes place at work and on the clock. But just how far can management go in attempting to control an employee's behavior away from the workplace? What arguments does the employer have to make for the arbitrator to agree that discipline is appropriate for off-duty conduct?

For management to be successful, it must convincingly argue that the employee's off-duty conduct conflicts with one of the employer's legitimate business interests. So union arguments need to focus on proving that the conduct did not or could not negatively impact the economic objectives of the employer. While each case must be decided on its own merits, there are some guidelines for examining whether what happens away from work will lead to discipline.

DID THE EMPLOYEE'S OFF-DUTY BEHAVIOR ADVERSELY AFFECT THE REPUTATION OR ECONOMIC INTERESTS OF THE EMPLOYER?

Grounds for discipline may include: threatening or harassing supervisors or co-workers; directly or indirectly harming the employer's product or service; competing with the employer; or violent, destructive or perverted actions.

Employers may use claims that the public knew about the employee's behavior because it was widely publicized and hurt the employer. Or the employer may claim that the injury to business will occur because the disciplined employee regularly deals face-to-face with the public. The greater the media coverage where the employee is identified, and the more serious the nature of the off-duty misconduct, the stronger management's potential case becomes.

To defend the worker, the union must have an accurate picture of just how widespread the news coverage was and whether the coverage clearly identified the employee. Only when the union knows the facts can it succeed in arguing that the employer is exaggerating the damage that the incident could cause to the business.

WAS THE EMPLOYEE NOT AVAILABLE OR ILL-SUITED TO PERFORM THE ASSIGNED WORK BECAUSE OF THE OFF-DUTY CONDUCT?

If an employee is arrested or incarcerated for a crime and cannot report for work, management may claim that business was damaged because productivity was hampered.

Discipline may, in some cases, depend upon the employee's job description, and the length of incarceration. Management must prove that the employee was of critical importance and that her absence created a hardship for the employer. In some instances, arbitrators have agreed that when an employee is charged with a theft, the employer has the right to remove the employee from a job entering homes—such as to read indoor utility meters—because he was ill-suited to perform the job.

In at least one instance, an arbitrator upheld a discharge where there was only the potential for a business loss. When a Baltimore bus driver was publicly identified as the acting Grand Dragon of the Ku Klux Klan, management argued that there was the potential for physical violence and an economic boycott of the bus company. The arbitrator agreed and upheld the discharge.

In order to be able to counter management's claims, unions need to be able to document what impact, if any, the employee's off-duty conduct or absence had on the employer's business.

CAN THE EMPLOYER SHOW THAT OTHER EMPLOYEES REFUSE TO WORK WITH THE EMPLOYEE OR ARE AT PERSONAL RISK AS A RESULT OF THE OFF-DUTY BEHAVIOR?

In cases where the behavior was so dangerous or perverted that co-workers want nothing to do with the employee, arbitrators have upheld discipline. Employers have a harder time with this argument when unions are able to show through the use of petitions or witnesses that the off-duty conduct has little or no effect on co-workers.

In all cases, management must be able to show a clear connection between the off-duty conduct and a harm to the employer's legitimate business interests. Where the employer cannot prove the connection, arbitrators are reluctant to uphold the discipline.

PERSONAL APPEARANCE

Dramatic changes in clothing, hair, grooming and jewelry styles over the past couple of decades have caused a lot of friction between workers and their employers. Stewards should understand that while employers typically have the right to establish reasonable rules, those rules should not require conformity simply for the sake of conformity.

Back in 1969, citing personal freedoms protected by the U.S. Constitution, the U.S. Seventh Circuit Court of Appeals sustained a worker's right to wear his hair at a length he chooses. If an employer wants to have a rule limiting that right, the employer has an obligation to show some business or safety reason to support it.

PUBLIC CONTACT IS KEY

If the worker is in a job that does not involve dealing with the public, then clothing (including uniforms), hair, body jewelry and personal cleanliness rules are not as easy to enforce—unless the employer can document complaints or negative remarks from fellow workers that the worker's appearance has an adverse effect on business.

The employer's personal appearance rules should be discussed in advance with the union. They should be published in advance of their effective date, should be stated clearly and should be understood by the people the rules affect. They should be posted on the bulletin board, or individuals should be personally notified so that they understand what grooming or uniform rules are in force.

NO DISCRIMINATION IS ALLOWED

It's difficult to enforce rules consistently where you have men and women, people of different ages or races, or where there is a considerable difference in the skills of the people covered by the rules. People working the night shift may get away with more than those on the more visible day shift. It is difficult to fire a man for wearing his hair long or wearing earrings if women can wear their hair long and wear earrings. African-American workers may choose to wear Afro, cornrow, dreadlock or other hair styles that are different from their white colleagues. All must be treated the same with regard to clothing and grooming to make a rule enforceable.

SAFETY AND HEALTH ARE LEGITIMATE ISSUES

Arbitrators usually support the employer if safety is involved, and the worker's grooming creates a risk to self or others. For example, this may arise if a worker has a beard or facial hair that interferes with the fit of a respirator, or where failing to follow rules on protective clothing exposes an employee to burns or physical injury.

Also, the union is on stronger ground if it can be shown that the employee made a repeated effort to conform to the rule but was disciplined anyway.

Additionally, if you can show that a worker will suffer personal harm or difficulty because of the rule's application, you may do better. Examples: someone of the Orthodox Jewish faith being required to cut his beard or side-locks, or any worker with

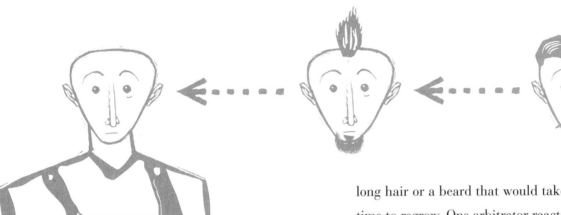

long hair or a beard that would take a long time to regrow. One arbitrator reacted sympathetically to a worker who furnished evidence that his romance would suffer if he were forced to shave and get a haircut.

HANDLING AN APPEARANCE CASE

When faced with a grievance in this area, stewards have a better chance of winning if they can show that their employer's grooming or clothing rule is extreme compared to other employers in the same industry. This may involve furnishing photographs, testimony by outsiders or possibly citing earlier arbitration cases to help establish the union's point.

DUE PROCESS MUST BE FOLLOWED

In any event, the punishment given out should follow the normal grievance process. In most contracts that usually means a verbal warning (or counseling), written warning, suspension, and only as a last resort, discharge.

The public's attitude toward nonconformity has changed a lot over the past thirty years. Since the 1960s, we have come a long way toward accepting diversity in appearance, as long as it does not tread on the toes of fellow workers or the business interests of the employer. Just remember to make sure the workers for whom you are responsible get an even break.

JOB CLASSIFICATION

"I should be paid more for what I do!"

As a steward, you're likely to hear that complaint a lot. But doing something about it—getting a pay increase for someone—involves more than just going in and pounding on the table. Handling job classification grievances takes a little know-how.

A good place to begin is the employee's job description. If the duties being performed are spelled out, then the worker probably doesn't have a case, unless the union wasn't in on the original rate-setting process. But if the worker is performing important duties that require additional skill or responsibility and those duties are missing, then there's a chance that the description should be rewritten.

IS THERE A SYSTEM?

Next, check to see if there is a job evaluation system—a classification process—which covers bargaining unit jobs. If so, get a copy, find out what the compensable factors are, and see whether other comparable jobs have been evaluated and placed in higher pay grades.

Does your agreement mention job evaluation and are job study requests handled in a separate procedure? Ask the appropriate union official to take a look at the job with you. Get a copy of the job description and consult with the worker and supervisor to determine whether it is accurate.

If job evaluation isn't mentioned in the agreement, management may be using it to set rates anyway—the majority of workplaces have some kind of job evaluation. You're looking for the compensable factors. Remember that you're entitled to review guidelines last used to set pay or determine conditions of work, since those are areas that your union has a right to bargain over.

Check out the basis upon which pay decisions are made. Almost all job classification systems put the most weight on skill, which generally includes formal education as well as on-the-job experience. Next is responsibility, usually for tools and equipment, material and product, and work of others. Less important—but also considered—are physical and/or mental effort and working conditions, which includes both adverse surroundings and hazards on the job. To justify an upgrade, the union has to show that the job being performed involves significantly more skill, responsibility, effort or more adverse or dangerous working conditions than detailed in the job description.

MAKING THE EVALUATION REQUEST

In processing a request for an evaluation, the steward should determine if the job has changed, or if a significant duty was overlooked in the previous evaluation. For example: hiring new workers with significantly higher education levels or experience levels than originally required; operating complex machines that require more complicated planning or setups; or requiring substantially increased physical effort or mental concentration. These facts need to be brought to the attention of management.

In most workplaces you can generally count on management rejecting the first request for a reclassification. It takes pushing to get them to do their own study. The steward and worker need to be patient when requesting a reclassification and upgrade— but they also need to persevere.

MAKING AN EFFECTIVE PRESENTATION

The surest way to make an effective presentation is to compare the job that you think is underpaid with other, higher-paid jobs that carry the same levels of skill and responsibility.

Does the job you're comparing share many of the same duties of the job in question? But be aware that just because a worker has been asked to do one of the duties of a higher-paid job he's not necessarily entitled to the higher rate. It's the mix of duties that determines the rate of pay, not just one duty out of many.

For instance, if a worker is assigned to a computer terminal he isn't automatically entitled to an upgrade, since sometimes computers can actually make a job simpler and easier. Rather, find out whether the computer work is of a complex nature, such as writing new programs or modifying existing ones, as opposed to simply keying in a few numbers and then getting output on a computer monitor or printer.

On the other hand, some new jobs are far more complex than existing ones. Workers in those jobs might rate a higher pay level than existing workers, and a new pay level will have to be created. In that case, the steward may face controversy with the former highest-paid workers, who resent the presence of jobs that are acknowledged to be more skilled than their own.

Making sure that your co-workers are properly paid for their job skills and responsibilities is an important task of the steward, and stewards can be a vital link in the process of getting jobs properly classified.

5 HEALTH AND SAFETY ISSUES

The workplace is one of North America's most dangerous neighborhoods. Wherever you work and whatever you do, you face health and safety perils on the job. Hazards exist nearly everywhere, from indoor air pollution in office buildings to lead exposure on construction sites.

It's estimated that some one hundred thousand men and women die each year from occupational illness in the United States, and another ten to fifteen thousand die from on-the-job accidents or violence. That's like a jumbo jet crashing every day of the year.

We can't depend on the good will of employers to protect us; it's our job to look out for our own safety and that of our co-workers.

Occupational illnesses and injuries are preventable. In order to protect ourselves, we must be aware of and use the safety provisions of the contract and of the safety and health laws, and we must use our own good sense. For union stewards, a first step toward reducing injury and illness is to learn about the hazards particular to their job sites.

This chapter outlines some of the steward's rights and obligations, and pinpoints some of the most difficult safety and health problems in the workplace. Don't feel you have to become the total expert in this sometimes highly technical area. Don't hesitate to contact your national union for help. Another great national resource is the highly respected New York Committee for Occupational Safety and Health (NYCOSH), 275 Seventh Ave., New York, NY 10001. Phone: 212-627-3900.

WORKPLACE HEALTH AND SAFETY: THE BASICS

You don't have to be an ironworker or firefighter to face dangers on the job. Occupational safety and health hazards can be found in virtually every type of work setting. And because they are often hard to detect, many threats can go unrecognized until they become extremely dangerous. In some cases they can be fatal.

Some safety hazards are obvious, like unprotected floor openings on a construction site. But there are many others—like the uneven floor tile everyone keeps tripping over, or poor ventilation—that are so commonplace they can be easily forgotten or overlooked until they contribute to a major accident or illness. Health hazards, ranging from toxic solvents to extreme stress, are common everywhere, from factories to offices, from retail stores to hospitals.

To ensure that no hazard is taken for granted, every local union should strive to establish a safety and health committee to educate members about hazards on the job and to monitor safety conditions, pushing employers to take corrective action. But before stewards can effectively address these hazards, it's important to learn as much as possible about the kinds of dangers we all face. In the end, no law, no power, can protect us without our own informed, aggressive defense.

COMMON HEALTH HAZARDS

The thing about workplace health hazards is that they're not always obvious—and, in many cases, no one even knows there's a threat out there until damage has already been done. Following is a list of common hazards that stewards should be aware of.

Repetitive Strain

Cumulative trauma disorders (CTDs), including repetitive strain injuries (RSIs), now account for roughly 60 percent of all reported occupational illnesses in the United States. Computerization of offices has contributed to this skyrocketing rate, but the majority of CTDs still occur in manufacturing facilities. To prevent the kind of fast, repetitive movements and prolonged awkward postures that can cause CTDs, stewards should survey members to identify work areas and jobs where these types of injuries occur. Solutions can be complex, but will undoubtedly focus on ergonomics—the science of fitting the workplace to the worker, rather than forcing the worker to adapt to a harmful work pattern. Potential solutions include redesign of work stations, regular rest breaks and rotation of jobs.

Noise

Exposure to noise gradually wears down the nerves of the inner ear, and can cause both temporary and permanent hearing loss. Stewards should push management for noise level inspections; for development of plans to reduce noise by redesigning processes; and, while those engineering controls are being implemented, for the use of personal protective equipment.

Lighting

Poor lighting conditions can cause eye strain, headaches, blurred vision and an increase in accidents. Management should provide lighting appropriate to the work assignment, remembering that higher levels of light are necessary where contrast is low.

Stewards should be alert to the quality of light in different work areas—particularly the level of glare and contrast.

Radiation

Exposure to ionizing radiation (for example, x-rays) can result in a variety of adverse health effects, from cancers to birth defects. Although less is known about the effects of nonionizing radiation—found, among other places, in computer video display terminals—some scientists believe it, also, could result in adverse health effects. To reduce exposures, keep as much distance as possible from the source of radiation. (For computer users, levels drop dramatically two feet from video screens.)

Temperature Extremes

It may not seem unusually hot or cold where you work, but you may be so used to the temperature that it is easy to ignore. Yet temperature extremes can be very dangerous—and even fatal. Stewards can monitor the temperature by checking with members, and by measuring the workplace temperature either with a standard thermometer or with a globe thermometer, which also measures humidity and air movement.

Chemical Hazards

Chemicals can cause serious health problems for workers suffering high-level exposures. Stewards should know what chemicals come into the workplace and where they go. Using OSHA's Hazard Communication Standard, ask your employer for material safety data sheets (MSDSs) to learn about the health effects of each chemical. Then push either for removal of hazardous chemicals entirely, for substitution of safer chemical products or for changes in the work process. Employees have a right to know what hazardous materials they are exposed to.

Biological Hazards

Indoor air quality can be dramatically compromised if biological agents, such as bacteria, molds and spores, are allowed to grow and circulate within the workplace ventilation system. To prevent a variety of serious illnesses, ventilation systems should be checked regularly, as should locations that serve as breeding grounds for molds, spores and bacteria, such as water-damaged areas.

Stress

Many different job conditions can cause and aggravate stress in working men and women—job insecurity, production quotas, sexual harassment, shift work and isolation, among others. In general, stressful jobs usually have two common ingredients: high demands and little control. Stress produces both psychological and biological effects, including high blood pressure, elevated cholesterol levels, diabetes and emotional disorders such as depression. To help eliminate stress on the job, the causes must be eliminated. Strong contract language and grievance procedures can be good first steps. For example, an adequate staffing clause can alleviate stress caused by unfair job demands and insecurity.

COMMON SAFETY HAZARDS

While a lot of health hazards are largely invisible, some safety hazards are so visible and commonplace that they're not even noticed: workers get so used to these everyday situations that nobody thinks twice about them. Don't allow yourself and your people to become lulled into danger. Identifying a hazard and reporting it to management is an important health and safety function for a steward.

Housekeeping/Cleanliness

Watch out for dirty work surfaces covered with debris, which can cause serious slips, trips and falls. Also, make sure materials and equipment are stored properly to prevent them from falling on workers.

Walkways

Walkways and aisles should be wide enough for the task at hand, and elevated walkways should be guarded with railings. Aisles should be free of debris and in compliance with both local fire codes and OSHA fire regulations. Also keep an eye out for uneven or cracked flooring.

Lifting/Materials Handling

Jobs that involve lifting and pulling can cause serious health problems, including hernias and, of course, back trouble—the single largest workers' compensation expense in North America. Push for the use of mechanical lifting devices—fork lifts and hand trucks—whenever possible.

Machinery Guarding

Make sure that machines are properly guarded to prevent any possible contact between moving parts and the worker. Using unguarded machines violates federal safety regulations and can result in cuts and bruises, lost fingers and crushed bones.

Personal Protective Equipment

Ensure that the proper eyewear is provided in high-risk operations. Similarly, where appropriate, such basics as hard hats, safety lines, safety shoes and the like should be employed. (One of the OSHA

HEALTH AND SAFETY CHECKLIST

From office workers to construction workers and everything in between, we all do radically different kinds of work, but we're all candidates for injury or illness on the job. Here's a brief look at some of the biggest threats facing workers in a range of industries.

Auto Workers and Machinists
- Asbestos and abrasive dusts
- Brake fluids
- Carbon monoxide
- Gasoline
- Lead
- Noise
- Solvents

Communications
- Electromagnetic radiation (from computers and power lines)
- Cumulative trauma disorders (CTDs)
- Stress
- Trenching

Construction
- Adhesives
- Asbestos
- Back injuries
- CTDs
- Falls
- Gasoline
- Lead
- Man-made fibers
- Plastics
- Shoring and trenching
- Solvents

Food Industry
- Bleaches and detergents
- CTDs
- Heat and cold exposure
- Infections
- Insecticides

Garment Industry
- CTDs
- Dyes
- Fires
- Formaldehyde
- Soaps
- Solvents

Hospitals and Health Care
- Back injuries
- Disinfectants
- Drugs
- Infections
- Infectious disease
- Radiation

Offices
- CTDs
- Duplicating fluid and toner
- Electromagnetic radiation
- Indoor air pollution
- Vapors from new furnishings

Petrochemical Industry
- Aromatic hydrocarbons (carcinogens)
- Explosions
- Radiation
- Solvents

Postal Service
- Back injuries
- Carbon monoxide
- Dust
- Dermatitis
- CTDs

Steel Industry
- Arsenic
- Coke (lung cancer)
- Dust and vapors from exposure to heavy metals
- Heat exposure

Retailing
- Back injuries
- Indoor air pollution
- Infectious disease
- RSI
- Stress
- Violence

Public Transportation
- Carbon monoxide
- Diesel
- Exposure to heat and cold
- Noise
- Vibration
- Violence

Trucking and Warehousing
- Back injuries
- Carbon monoxide
- Diesel
- Exposure to heat and cold
- Noise
- Vibration

Utilities
- Asbestos
- Electromagnetic radiation
- Falls
- Polychlorinated biphenyls (PCBs)
- Lead
- Noise
- Scaffold hazards
- Welding

citations most commonly issued is for failure to provide personal protective gear.)

Lock-Out/Tag-Out

Any time a machine is repaired, it should be locked out to ensure that electricity is shut off. This means more than just pulling the plug: it means making sure, through use of a safety mechanism or other control, that the machine cannot be put into operation while an unsuspecting repair worker is attending to it. And it means visibly tagging the machine to warn of danger.

Hand Tools

Slippery handles, dull blades and loose pieces can inadvertently turn hand tools into hazards—especially in a crowded work area.

Electrical Hazards

According to the National Institute for Occupational Safety and Health (NIOSH), electrical malfunction is the leading cause of all fires. Exposed metal parts and wiring can cause shocks when used near water, or if the machinery is poorly maintained; electrical shorts are especially hazardous. Make sure that all equipment is grounded or double-insulated; that switch boxes and circuit boxes are properly labeled; and that circuit breakers and fuses are clearly marked.

Fire/Explosions

Watch out for blocked or locked exits and unsafe storage of flammable material. In addition, make sure all exits are marked and paths are uncluttered, and that fire extinguishers and sprinklers have been inspected recently.

First Aid/Emergency Response

Of course, every workplace should have a plan for how to respond to emergencies, as well as basic first aid equipment, such as bandages and antiseptic. When an emergency happens, a steward with knowledge of exit routes, fire alarms and extinguishers, and other emergency response considerations can be a valuable asset.

WORKER PROTECTIONS UNDER LAW

After years of struggle, the labor movement has won certain basic safety and health rights for working people. Some of these rights are mandated by federal laws—such as the Occupational Safety and Health Act—while others are spelled out in contract language.

Stewards should note that health and safety rights do not guarantee a workplace free of hazards. However, when workers are

educated about basic safety and health protections, including laws and contract language, they can begin to use these tools to push management to clean up the work environment.

It is also important to remember that OSHA covers all private sector workers and federal government employees, and state plans cover public employees in twenty-three states. However, 7.5 million public workers in the remaining twenty-seven states have no legal OSHA rights.

Stewards should become familiar with the following safety and health rights, which apply to all public or private sector workers:

☞ The right to obtain safety and health information from your employer, including information about chemical hazards, workplace air testing or medical testing. This right is mandated under OSHA's Hazard Communication Standard, as well as the National Labor Relations Act.

☞ The right to bring outside experts into the workplace to conduct walk-through inspections and evaluations. This is a provision of the NLRA, but it can be strengthened by negotiating contract language as well.

☞ The right to be free from discrimination for exercising health and safety rights, such as the refusal of unsafe work. This is a right under both OSHA and the NLRA, but stewards should note that discrimination cases must be carefully documented.

☞ The right to establish union health and safety committees. A strong health and safety committee provides the first line of defense against hazards on the job. This right should be negotiated in all union contracts.

In addition to the above rights, the following rights apply to workers covered by OSHA:

☞ The right to a workplace free of recognized hazards. This fundamental right is mandated under OSHA's General Duty Clause. (Stewards should check with their local or national union's safety and health department about how it can be applied.)

☞ The right to training about chemicals you work with, their hazards and how to work with them safely. This is your right to know—a cornerstone of OSHA.

☞ The right to participation in meetings between OSHA and management to contest the length of time employers

are given to correct OSHA violations. If unions are unaware of this right, OSHA may agree to allow management more time than may be safe to abate the hazard.

☞ The right to accompany OSHA inspectors while they are conducting an investigation of your workplace. This allows workers, who know better than anyone the hazards where they work, the right to participate in OSHA inspections.

OSHA'S GENERAL DUTY CLAUSE

If you're faced with a serious threat to health and safety, don't feel you've got to go running to the law books so you can quote chapter and verse to the boss. All you need to remember is OSHA's General Duty Clause: "Each employer shall furnish to each of his employees employment and a place of employment which are free from recognized hazards that are causing or are likely to cause death or serious physical harm to his employees." (Section 5 of the Occupational Safety and Health Act, Public Law 91-596)

☛ The right to participate in hearings between OSHA and your employer regarding a management request for a variance. This provides the union with an opportunity to ensure that employer-requested variances from OSHA standards provide as much protection as the standard itself.

☛ The right to petition OSHA for new standards. Because OSHA regulates only about five hundred of the estimated sixty thousand chemicals in use throughout American workplaces, and a limited number of unsafe work conditions, this is an important right that should be utilized by unions to demand swift passage of regulations for the most hazardous substances.

In addition, stewards should know about reporting procedures, such as OSHA Form 200, a list of all reported on-the-job injuries and illnesses. Workplaces covered by OSHA are required to publicly post a Form 200 every February. Upon request, employers must also make a copy of the full log of workplace health and safety incidents available throughout the year.

Unions can use this log to target unsafe areas—"risk-mapping"—and bargain for better conditions. The information can also be used to find out where the most injuries and illnesses occur, or to find out what type of injuries or illnesses occur most frequently.

YOUR RIGHT TO KNOW

The Occupational Safety and Health Administration's Hazard Communication Standard (HCS) requires employers to provide workers with information on all toxic substances they may be exposed to on the job. It's a valuable tool that can be used by stewards to strengthen health and safety protections for workers everywhere.

The purpose of the standard is to ensure that workers who may be exposed to dangerous chemicals know the risks involved and understand how to prevent any illness or injury the chemicals might cause. Although the HCS originally applied only to the manufacturing industry, it now covers all worksites.

The standard has five essential elements that stewards should understand. According to the law, employers must:

☛ Train employees before they work with dangerous chemicals, and whenever new substances are introduced into the workplace.

☛ Put appropriate labels on containers

holding hazardous chemicals, identifying any toxic substances and providing warnings as appropriate.

☞ Provide access at the worksite to material safety data sheets (MSDSs)— fact sheets about a particular chemical or group of chemicals workers may be exposed to.

☞ Develop and make available to workers a written hazard communication program. This includes a plan for employer compliance with the law, a list of hazardous substances and methods for informing workers.

☞ Furnish information on the effects and properties of chemicals, even if the chemical name is withheld because it's a trade secret.

Although one in four workers is exposed to chemical hazards on the job today, most employers virtually ignore the HCS. According to OSHA, tens of thousands of violations of the standard have occurred since it went into effect in late 1985, and millions of dollars in fines are levied every year.

Hazard Communication Standard violations are treated the same as any federal health and safety violation. Upon request, your area OSHA office will send you a complaint form to complete. (Names are kept confidential and complainants are protected by law from harassment.) Unions also have the right to:

☞ Ask employers for a copy of their written program, a schedule for training and MSDS forms for information about particular chemicals in your workplace.

☞ Use the HCS along with the OSHA Access to Medical Records Standard to obtain all the information an employer has, including monitoring records and the results of any medical testing.

☞ Use this information to support members' compensation claims or personal injury lawsuits.

☞ File grievances and push for stronger contract language.

☞ Develop a "Ten Most Wanted List" of toxic chemicals, and try to replace these chemicals with less harmful substances.

Some states have their own right-to-know laws, and in a few cases they offer more protection than the federal Hazard Communication Standard. For information about right-to-know laws in your area, call your state AFL-CIO. For more information about the OSHA standard itself, contact your union's safety and health department.

CONFRONTING DANGEROUS ASSIGNMENTS

Every day, workers across North America are assigned to dangerous jobs that could seriously hurt or even kill them. It is vitally important for every steward to know how to respond when workers are confronted with these situations.

Recognize that the law is lousy and was written to benefit employers rather than employees, and thus there is only limited legal protection for workers who refuse to perform potentially unsafe jobs. As a result, workers taking this step need to understand very clearly that they are putting their jobs on the line.

It is true that workers have won a very restricted right under the law to refuse hazardous work, but that right applies only when the conditions of the situation meet very specific requirements. Consequently, your union's collective bargaining agreement is the best vehicle for winning the right to refuse.

A contract can include a variety of provisions for stopping an unsafe job, including statements of the employer's duty to provide a safe workplace and the union's right to refuse hazardous work. It's also legal to have a clause outlining protection against discharge for workers who exercise their right to refuse.

If a worker in your shop has no alternative but to refuse a hazardous job—and if your union contract does not include a work refusal procedure—follow these steps:

☛ Make sure the union knows what's going on.

☛ Talk to all the workers affected by the hazard. It will strengthen the union's position if there is collective action.

☛ Promptly notify your supervisor of the hazard, making it clear that there is imminent danger.

☛ Do not actually refuse the work. Accept it on the condition that the job is made safe. In addition, inform your employer that, in the meantime, you will perform other work.

☛ Do not leave the job site unless ordered to by your employer.

☛ Call OSHA and demand an *imminent danger* inspection if your employer fails to immediately correct the hazard.

In the event someone is discharged for refusing a dangerous assignment, there are three strategies stewards can use to reinstate that worker:

- ☛ File a discrimination complaint under Section 11(c) of OSHA.
- ☛ File an unfair labor practice charge with the National Labor Relations Board.
- ☛ Most important, use your union's grievance procedure, arguing that the employer did not have just cause to discharge the worker.

CUMULATIVE TRAUMA DISORDERS

Stamping price tags on 7,000 garments per day, performing the same weld on 101 cars every hour, gutting a chicken every two seconds, entering 15,000 keystrokes of data every hour, sewing cuffs on 1,500 shirts each day.

From cool, computer-filled offices to sweltering garment shops, labor is systematically being reduced to dull, repetitive and often dangerous tasks. While business-es are reaping huge benefits, workers in many industries are performing jobs that are numbingly repetitive and potentially crippling.

Cumulative trauma disorders, including repetitive strain injuries (RSIs), are a group of health problems resulting from overuse or misuse of muscles, tendons and nerves. At first barely noticeable, the symptoms may become so severe that victims have difficulty with the simplest tasks, like opening a jar or operating a vacuum cleaner. In fact, CTDs are now the number-one cause of occupational illness in the United States. Stewards need to know how to recognize work conditions that can lead to these illnesses and how to identify early signs of CTDs.

Although the human body is able to adapt to a variety of different physical situations, it does have limits—and sustained awkward postures and repetitive tasks can often push workers way over the edge. According to the science known as ergonomics, the workplace should be

designed to fit workers; workers shouldn't have to contort themselves to fit poorly designed jobs. Stewards should be on the lookout for the five biggest risk factors for CTDs: rapid and repetitive motion; awkward postures; forceful motions; lack of control over the pace of work; and vibration (usually caused by machinery). Other factors that can contribute to CTDs include working in cold temperatures, job stress and inadequate rest breaks.

Early detection and medical treatment of CTDs can prevent development of serious and sometimes crippling problems. Furthermore, research also shows that a properly designed workplace can dramatically reduce the frequency of CTDs.

Early detection depends on recognizing the variety of CTD symptoms that occur.

COMMON COMPLAINTS FROM CTD VICTIMS

- ☛ Aching
- ☛ Numbness
- ☛ Tenderness
- ☛ Swelling
- ☛ Loss of strength
- ☛ Pain
- ☛ Tingling
- ☛ Loss of joint movement
- ☛ Decreased coordination

Among the most frequently occurring CTDs are carpal tunnel syndrome, which affects the nerves and tendons of the wrists and fingers; bursitis, which affects the muscles and tendons in the shoulder; and tendinitis—inflammation of the tendons.

Because early treatment greatly increases the chances of a successful recovery, it helps to get medical attention as soon as possible. A proper medical exam should include taking down a thorough medical and work history, a physical exam (including tests to determine the victim's "range of motion"), and diagnostic testing (depending on the severity and nature of the problem). In some cases, it may be necessary for a health professional to observe the worker performing his or her job.

Victims should be encouraged to ask the union to recommend a doctor or health clinic with experience treating CTDs, and for assistance filing for workers' compensation. Physical therapy is frequently the most effective treatment. Surgery should be a last resort.

Stewards who see potential problems in their workplaces should ask their union safety and health department to conduct an ergonomic assessment of the workplace to determine what conditions might cause CTDs. If the working conditions are not changed, CTDs will continue to occur and recur.

Such a workplace survey should focus on both the design of the tools and equipment used in the job and the design of the job tasks. Equipment should be designed to enable people of different heights and weights to perform tasks comfortably, and in many cases this may require adjustable work stations. The design of job tasks should incorporate proper pacing, adequate rest breaks and duration of the job. If the survey's results indicate a high rate of complaints, you can publicize the results in your newsletter.

Pushing management to improve work conditions may not be easy. There is currently no specific standard regulating those conditions—OSHA's plans to set some basic guidelines have so far fallen victim to a combination of intense employer lobbying and a corporate-friendly Congress.

Work with your union safety and health department to develop strategies for improving things. Some unions have succeeded in securing strong contract language providing protection for members from CTDs.

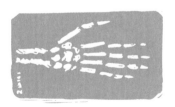

Indoor air pollution is a major occupational health problem. Contamination of indoor air occurs when toxic substances combine with poor ventilation to cause health problems ranging from minor eye, nose and throat irritations to life-threatening respiratory infections.

Poor air quality can be traced to many sources, including office equipment, new furnishings, carpeting and construction materials. In addition, buildings are often designed or renovated without attention to proper ventilation, resulting in sealed windows, blocked vents and a general lack of fresh air. Even when proper ventilation exists, however, building owners and employers often try to save the cost of heating and cooling air by recirculating stale air, which exposes workers to a variety of contaminants.

Because your employer may not own the building you work in—and because there are no government laws or regulations that force building owners to provide adequate air—indoor air quality can be one of the most frustrating job-related health problems to tackle. Keep in mind that solutions are often possible, but be careful: blame can quickly be shifted onto the union if expectations are raised and problems go unsolved.

To begin, you can push for an increased supply of fresh air and ongoing procedures for cleaning and maintaining the ventilation system. You can also demand an inspection by a ventilation engineer, and implementation of his or her recommendations.

If your employer (or the building owner) is unwilling to cooperate, unions can consider the following steps:

☞ Conduct a health survey of the members, looking for symptoms tied to indoor air problems.

☞ Investigate the ventilation system. Hold tissue paper near vents to see if they're working and make sure each room has both an intake vent and an exhaust vent.

☞ Based on the survey and investigation, develop recommendations for improving air quality.

☞ With the help of a union health and safety expert, write contract language to protect your rights to clean air.

AIR QUALITY REPORT

STEVE MAGNUSON

AIDS IN THE WORKPLACE

More than three hundred thousand Americans are known to have died of AIDS. Many workers are extremely afraid of contracting the disease on the job. Some are even afraid of working alongside people who are infected, or who they think are infected. Who is at risk? What can those workers do to protect themselves?

Working men and women may be exposed to HIV (the virus that causes AIDS) on the job only if they have contact with contaminated blood, semen or vaginal secretions. Workers potentially at risk include hospital and health care personnel, corrections officers, mental health workers, emergency response personnel, laboratory workers, mortuary attendants and custodians.

Fears of AIDS are real, and every effort should be made by the union to clear up any misinformation and to educate people about the risks. In the workplace, HIV infections are transmitted in only a few specific ways:

☛ Accidental needle stick wounds.
☛ Splashing of large quantities of infected blood in the eyes or mouth.
☛ Having infected blood come into contact with damaged skin.

At the same time, men and women afraid to work with co-workers who are infected with HIV should also be educated about how these viruses are *not* transmitted. Close, nonsexual contact causes no risk. Coughing, sneezing, eating together, using the same telephone, sharing restrooms or shaking hands *cannot* transmit the disease. Of the more than 500,000 reported cases of AIDS in the United States, according to the federal Centers for Disease Control and Prevention, not a single case has been documented to have been transmitted by saliva, tears or sweat.

Accurate information is the most important preventive measure. Some unions have successfully proposed joint labor/management education programs, taught by trained professionals. But whatever the strategy, it is vital that stewards dispel any myths about AIDS in the workplace.

For workers at risk of exposure, some specific precautions have been recommended by the CDC, including the following:

☛ Use gloves for any contact with contaminated blood or fluids.
☛ Wear gowns, masks and goggles during procedures where splashes of blood or fluid might occur.
☛ Dispose of used needles in an

approved puncture-proof container.

☛ Use mouthpieces or other safety devices for mouth-to-mouth resuscitation.

RADIATION ALERT

You don't have to work in a nuclear power plant or be a medical x-ray technician to be concerned about the hazards of radiation, which, with intense exposure, is a known cause of cancer. Stewards in a variety of jobs should be particularly aware of the potential risks of a less-than-obvious source of danger, electromagnetic radiation.

Few people are familiar with the potential dangers posed by electromagnetic radiation, or EMR. This form of radiation is emitted from a wide variety of electronic equipment and installations, posing a potential threat to computer users, workers on power lines and others.

Although there is no conclusive evidence linking EMR and cancer, it remains a prime suspect. Much is still not known, but recent scientific surveys indicate that long-term exposure may contribute to miscarriages, and some evidence suggests that EMR may play a role in a rare cancer found in a small number of children. In response

to this evidence, more and more unions are fighting for and winning contract language to safeguard against exposure to EMR.

Electromagnetic radiation describes both electric and magnetic fields given off by power lines, computer terminals and many common household items such as electric blankets and coffee makers. Electric and magnetic fields are measured separately, but both are potential health hazards.

Men and women required to work in electric or magnetic fields—including electricians and power line workers—may be at particular risk.

VIDEO DISPLAY TERMINALS

Some men and women are in front of computer video display terminals thirty-five hours a week or more. In addition to blurred vision, back pain and headaches, many workers are concerned about possible reproductive hazards. Can VDTs cause miscarriages and birth defects?

No one knows for sure, but it's possible. Some research suggests a link between VDT work and problem pregnancies. A 1988 California study, for example, showed that women using VDTs more than twenty hours per week were more than twice as likely to suffer a miscarriage as nonworking women. There's general agreement that if women are at risk, men are likely to be as well.

Unions are responding to real and potential VDT problems in a variety of ways—proposing transfers to non-VDT work during pregnancy, for example, and bargaining for purchase of proper furniture and lighting equipment, health and safety training, and fifteen-minute rest breaks for every two hours of computer use.

While we wait for more research and for the federal government to follow Sweden's lead and impose prudent limits on these emissions, there are a handful of precautions that stewards can take:

☞ Learn more about electromagnetic fields and educate co-workers.

☞ Examine existing health records, which employers must provide under OSHA regulation (29 CFR 1910.20). Also conduct health surveys to find out who is working in high-risk areas.

☞ Negotiate with management. More and more union contracts are addressing the threat of electromagnetic radiation, including agreements over VDT safety won by the Writers Guild of America and municipal employees in New York City. These include workstation design clauses and provisions for limiting the amount of time workers are at computer stations.

☞ Use good judgment and follow a policy of prudent avoidance. Try to limit exposure to potential radiation by moving people as far as possible away from its source. Since the intensity of these fields is dramatically reduced the farther away they are, try to keep a distance of at least three to four feet between a worker and the back of a computer monitor.

THE HEAT IS ON

For working men and women toiling under hot, humid conditions, heat is more than just irritating—it's dangerous.

Hot weather means hot workplaces, whether you're in a factory, on a construction site or in a laundry or office. During periods of extreme heat, many workers will suffer painful cramps, exhaustion and, in some cases, death.

The disturbing truth is that heat exposure in the workplace often exceeds that found in the hottest natural climates. Furthermore, heavy work can compromise any worker's capacity to endure high temperatures.

To help take the heat off workers, stewards should know the classic signs of heat stress:

- **Heat rash.** Caused by blockage of sweat glands, appears as a large patch of tiny red blister-like bumps—the same as prickly heat.

- **Dehydration.** Occurs when water lost through sweating is not replaced. Symptoms include thirst, loss of appetite, weakness, difficulty swallowing, muscle fatigue and, if untreated, shock.

- **Heat cramps**. Also a result of excessive sweating, occurs after lost body salt is not replaced. Symptoms include cramps in legs, arms and abdomen.

- **Heat exhaustion.** Caused by poor blood supply to the brain as a result of blood flowing to the skin's surface. Symptoms include fatigue, headache, nausea, moist and clammy skin, pale complexion and fainting.

- **Heat stroke.** A result of a dramatic increase in body temperature. Symptoms are body temperature of 106 degrees or greater; hot, dry skin surface with red, matted appearance; confusion, delirium, loss of consciousness and, if untreated, coma.

Although no government standards regulate temperature extremes in the workplace, stewards can take other steps to beat the heat. For temporary relief, workers should be advised to wear loose-fitting clothing (preferably cotton); drink a lot of cool water; wrap a wet cloth around the neck; and, when sweating heavily, take salt tablets.

Stewards can also monitor conditions by talking to co-workers—always the best method for measuring hazardous working conditions. If any workers are suffering from the symptoms mentioned above, it is either too hot in the workplace or adequate protection is not being provided. In addition, stewards can measure the workplace temperature either with an ordinary thermometer or a wet globe thermometer, which measures the total heat picture—air temperature, humidity and air movement. (Note that it can be effective to do this very conspicuously, so that management is aware the heat is being monitored.)

But if you want to do more than just treat the symptoms of heat stress, you can't do it alone. Develop a strategy to fight for safer conditions during hot days. Some recommendations for reducing the dangers of heat stress include engineering controls (fans, air conditioners, ventilation, protective equipment, isolating hot equipment); work practices (water, rest breaks, acclimatization, work in the coolest part of the day); and training (treatment of heat stress).

If the heat can no longer be tolerated and management balks at attempts to negotiate improvements, your union can stage a "chill-out." For a day or more, people report to work but stay in the coolest area of the workplace—maybe the cafeteria. This tactic can effectively pressure management to take steps to improve conditions. In one case, an employer responded by sending workers home for two weeks without pay while work was conducted to improve the temperature. However, workers successfully filed for unemployment, arguing that the company had laid them off—and working conditions were once again tolerable.

There are other tactics, as well. Be sure to work with your local union officers before trying anything too confrontational.

Remember, for bargaining, that union health and safety departments can often offer contract language that spells out procedures management must take on particularly hot days. The agreement may specify a temperature above which workers will not have to work.

Exposure to two of the most commonplace minerals on earth, lead and asbestos, has been found to be potentially life-threatening. Stewards should be on the lookout for possible exposures in their workplaces.

OMNIPRESENT ASBESTOS

Asbestos, which can cause cancer, asbestosis and other serious ailments, can turn up most anywhere: factories, offices, schools, you name it. For decades, it was the most common insulating material used.

No one can identify asbestos just by looking at it. A sample should be taken of the suspect material and it must be tested in a laboratory. Assume it is asbestos until proven otherwise and insist on protective equipment, monitoring and other safeguards.

Stewards facing potential asbestos problems should familiarize themselves with OSHA's asbestos standard. Among other things, the standard says that if asbestos is present, management must measure the amount that employees are breathing to determine if the levels are above permissible exposure limits. Keep in mind, though, that there is no such thing as a safe level of exposure.

GET THE LEAD OUT

Workers in more than one hundred occupations face potential lead exposure, which can cause health problems ranging from dizziness and memory lapse to reproductive hazards, brain damage and even death. Parents can expose children by coming home from work with lead on their clothing.

The OSHA Lead Standard provides workers with specific rights, including the right to medical tests, protective clothing and respirators, safe work practices, exposure monitoring, and training. Management's failure to provide any of the rights guaranteed by OSHA can be met with both a grievance and a complaint to OSHA. Unions can also use the standard as a bargaining tool to get management to resolve existing problems and to provide protection extending beyond the limits of the regulation.

THE RISKS OF SHIFT WORK

In a society demanding twenty-four-hour service as well as mass production, a growing number of people have jobs that require some form of shift work. This work includes graveyard, night, swing (evening) or rotating shifts, and it's not confined to steel mills, auto plants, oil refineries and coal mines. Today, shift work is commonplace in many service industries, such as health care and communications, as well as in retail operations and offices.

While the time clock where you work may keep ticking twenty-four hours a day, your own biological clock has a tough time keeping pace. People who work at night almost always have difficulty adjusting to this schedule, whether they work graveyard, swing or rotating shifts. These men and women are much more vulnerable to workplace accidents, and they suffer a wide variety of health problems, including increased incidence of heart disease, stomach disorders, insomnia, and in women, menstrual problems.

HOW THE BODY REACTS

The body functions at peak performance during the day, and its twenty-four-hour biological (or circadian) rhythms drop to their low point during the night. This internal clock is influenced by light and dark, night and day, and by what everyone else is doing around us. In turn, these rhythms influence a number of bodily functions, including temperature, heart rate, blood pressure and hormone levels.

During the graveyard shift, the circadian cycle is reversed: in effect, day becomes night. Under this grueling schedule, peak work demands come at the absolute low point of the body's biological rhythms, a time meant for rest and reduced activity.

Of all the types of shift work, rotating shifts are the worst, particularly if rotations occur as frequently as every week. But whether the schedule changes weekly or every six months, rotating shifts allow little opportunity for the body to adjust. This is especially true if the rotation does not "follow the sun" by moving workers from day to swing shift, or from swing to graveyard.

Making matters worse for shift workers, the day-night rhythm of the body is very slow to change. It is estimated that it takes at least one month of night-shift work for the body to completely reverse its normal functions. And even a small interruption in the schedule of shift workers, such as a weekend off, can fully revert the body to its normal pattern—a prescription for health problems as soon as the night shift begins again.

Making things even worse yet, when the body is out of rhythm and under stress or strain, many experts believe, it is more susceptible to the ill effects of hazardous conditions.

WHAT CAN UNIONS DO?

Ideally, for the workplace to be safe and for workers to be healthy, there should be no mandatory shift work. But the reality is that shift work is here to stay and working evenings and nights is a fact of life for many people. As a result, shift work should be given first to workers who volunteer. Meanwhile, unions should fight for straight or fixed shifts as opposed to rotating shifts. (If rotating shifts become mandatory, unions should push management to include a minimum of forty-eight hours off between shift changes.)

Unions and stewards should be aware of the health hazards of shift work and should push management to allow:

☛ A greater say in designing flexible work and shift schedules, and choice of shifts. (Some large industrial unions have negotiated contract clauses that give shift preference to workers with the greatest seniority. These preferences are often negotiated by the month.)

☛ First aid and medical services available twenty-four hours.

☛ Improved meal and transportation facilities.

☛ Training about hazards specifically related to shift work.

MINIMIZING THE PROBLEMS

In the meantime, here are a few tips for minimizing the problems that accompany shift work:

☛ Sleep in a dark, quiet room on as regular a schedule as possible.

☛ As you approach a change in shift, begin your adjustment by going to bed and getting up a bit later.

☛ Avoid taking medications to help you sleep or remain awake. Minimize your intake of sugar, caffeine and alcohol.

☛ Eat lightly before sleeping.

WORKPLACE VIOLENCE

As all too many stewards have learned, the threat of violence in today's society does not stop outside the walls of our workplaces. In fact, according to the Department of Labor, on-the-job homicides are the number-two cause of occupational death in the United States—and the number-one cause for women.

That's just part of the story. Millions of other public and private sector workers are victims of nonfatal but still violent incidents that occur at work, from emergency room nurses attacked by patients to grocery store clerks hurt during robberies. Countless other workers are harassed and threatened.

It is a scary issue for everyone. That's why it is especially important for stewards to learn how to recognize the signs of a potentially violent workplace and to know what can be done to minimize risks.

Identifying workplace violence is an important first step. Understand that it doesn't have to be outright physical assault to be violence: it can also be near misses, verbal abuse, sexual harassment or the threat of any of these. Even when a worker suffers no visible harm, the fear of violence can cause severe stress, which in itself can cause serious health problems.

While many workers are not at a particularly high risk, the number of those who are is rising. According to the National Institute for Occupational Safety and Health, factors that can increase a worker's risk of assaults in a workplace include:

☛ Working with the public.

☛ Working alone.

☛ Handling money.

☛ Coming in contact with patients or clients who may be violent.

☛ Being inexperienced.

Poor management can lead directly to

many of these high-risk conditions. Specific management-controlled factors that may add to the risk of a violent workplace include staff reductions (forcing people to work in isolation or without sufficient help), lack of training for workers about recognizing and handling violent situations, and failure to provide adequate emergency procedures.

While every employer should have a safety and security program, few do—even those workplaces vulnerable to violence. Stewards can therefore play an important role in organizing members to fight for safer workplaces that are free from assault incidents.

Here are three steps stewards can take toward reducing the potential for assaults in the workplace.

LISTEN UP

Talk to co-workers as much as possible about their safety concerns, just as you would talk about other hazards. Stewards might want to develop a short survey and distribute it throughout the workplace. It is also important to encourage members to document assault incidents, threats and harassment. In addition, keep everyone informed about specific problems.

MAKE A PLAN

Employers are obligated to protect workers from assault, but often they haven't considered the problem in a serious way and will likely be resistant to solutions. Stewards can help form safety committees to develop strategies for reducing the risk of violence. After gathering documentation of the problems, bring your complaint to management and propose concrete solutions. If your demands are met, publicize your victory.

GRIEVE, BARGAIN, AGITATE

If your complaint is ignored, you may want to consult with your local union officers about pursuing one or more of the following strategies:

- ☛ File a grievance.
- ☛ Refuse to work alone.
- ☛ For private sector workers and those covered by public employee safety and health plans, contact OSHA or your state safety enforcement agency and demand an inspection (even though there is no specific standard regulating exposure to workplace violence, OSHA has broad authority to penalize employers who do not provide a safe work environment).
- ☛ Publicize the problem in local media.
- ☛ Create a slogan campaign like Understaffing Kills. Wear the slogan on buttons, use it on bulletin board posters.
- ☛ Negotiate violence-prevention language in your next contract.

PHOTO: SUPERSTOCK

6 BUILDING UNITY AND STRENGTH

MOBILIZING YOUR CO-WORKERS/110

Four key elements in rallying your troops—the solution to making your job easier and the union stronger.

RECRUITING AND KEEPING VOLUNTEERS/112

Step-by-step, how to get rank-and-filers to help with every kind of union assignment—and get them back again and again.

CREATING UNIONISTS, NOT JUST MEMBERS/117

Your critical first steps when a new worker comes on the job.

THE RIGHT-TO-WORK CHALLENGE/119

Ways to build membership in right-to-work and open-shop states.

USING PRESSURE TO SETTLE GRIEVANCES/121

Tactics designed to help you win—way short of arbitration.

HELPING WIN BETTER CONTRACTS/123

What stewards can do to strengthen the union's hand at the bargaining table.

RALLYING THE TROOPS WITH LAUGHTER AND SONG/125

Humorous, easy-to-prepare skits and songs can help unite co-workers and focus their energies. Here's how to do it.

YES, IT WORKS!/129

Examples of how smart stewards and motivated members one-upped management and won their fights.

Almost every task a steward is called on to handle can be made easier with the support of co-workers—the more support, the better.

The plain truth is that supervisors treat stewards with more respect if it's clear they are really speaking not just for themselves but for dozens of others. With a united workforce, grievances are resolved more quickly and fairly—or never have to be filed in the first place. With a united workforce, the union is stronger at the bargaining table. And with a united workforce, when the union needs something done, stewards have co-workers to call on for assistance.

Achieving that unity and solidarity can be hard—perhaps the hardest task a steward faces. It's vitally important, though, and there are ways to bring it about. This chapter offers some ways to unite your troops and ways to exercise the power that flows from the strength of unity.

MOBILIZING YOUR CO-WORKERS

Mobilizing your co-workers involves four key steps: organizing, educating, targeting an issue and taking collective action.

ORGANIZING

Stewards have to be organized if they expect to organize others. That means you should maintain up-to-date information on each worker you're responsible for: membership status, job title, seniority date and a record of participation in past union activities. If you're responsible for more than twenty workers, you could recruit one or more mobilizers to help. Mobilization implies quick and effective communication with the members, and twenty is probably the effective limit.

EDUCATING

Workplace education is the driving force for mobilization that works, and presenting information for discussion is vital to this process. Information must flow both ways to be effective.

One-on-one education is a good place to start. The steward or mobilizer systematically contacts every worker in her area, presents the information or material and discusses the issue. This discussion should be planned and scheduled. For most issues, ten or fifteen minutes per worker should be enough, with some of the time reserved for questions and discussion. Don't lecture: the information being passed along should be all that's needed to inspire action.

Work group meetings might also be

considered, during worktime if your contract allows it. If you can't meet on the employer's time you can have a "Lunch with a Bunch"—turn the lunch break into a meeting. Distribute an agenda beforehand to generate attendance and ideas, and allow at least half the time for discussion and consideration of any action plan you want to pursue. Participation and discussion are the keys here.

ISSUES TARGETING

With good organization and education, workplace mobilization can be used in a wide variety of ways. In addition to providing support for contract bargaining or key grievances, it can be an effective tool to deal with concerns such as health and safety, changes in hours or shifts, the use of temporary or contract labor, unrealistic production quotas or national union issues such as health care or saving Social Security.

Issues that affect nearly everyone are the best ones around which to mobilize. Difficult issues shouldn't be avoided, but you should have some sense that unity is possible before you tackle something. If the issue is complex, it's often helpful to distribute a fact sheet before discussion. A simple list of the basic facts is sometimes most effective, and it's faster to produce.

COLLECTIVE ACTION

Good organization and education produce the unity necessary for effective collective action. Understand that such action need not mean confrontation with management. Initial action around an issue might begin with an intensive internal organizing drive to further develop unity in the workplace. Or initial action might begin with a petition drive. If an overwhelming majority of workers do not sign the petition, it can always be discarded or reviewed in a workplace meeting.

Remember when considering an action plan that each action should unite nearly every worker who agrees on the issue. Actions should escalate from solidarity actions, which are just demonstrations of unity, to more confrontational actions when necessary. The appropriate action will depend on the issue of the moment.

Take, for example, sick leave policy. You might begin with a member petition, followed by requesting a group meeting with management. If that fails, members could stage a sick-in, arriving at work wearing bandages or other sick-room paraphernalia. The next step might be a five-minute stand-up where everyone continues to work but stands together at their work station at an appointed time.

A LITTLE CAUTION

Consider the likely response from management before rushing ahead. Actions should demonstrate resolve and resistance but not be overly provocative. Persistence, continuing commitment and even repetition are usually crucial. Be sure you allow enough time between actions for management to implement a change in policy. Escalate only if management doesn't respond.

Obviously, confrontational actions require support and consultation with local union leaders. You could do more damage than good by charging off on your own.

Mobilizing at the workplace involves hard work but it can provide you with a renewed sense of commitment and energy. For many stewards, isolation and even powerlessness are replaced by real excitement as the members realize that the union is only as strong as their own involvement.

RECRUITING AND KEEPING VOLUNTEERS

A tree is only as strong as its roots, and a union is only as strong as its actively involved members. Just as unions couldn't function without stewards, unions also need member-volunteers to work on all sorts of committees, task forces, member surveys, petition campaigns, direct actions and more.

Members who are apathetic about the union are rarely, if ever, apathetic about other parts of their lives. It's just that they have a limited amount of time and guard it jealously.

"I have to pick up the kids after school."

"I've got a class that night."

"I have bowling on Wednesdays."

"I'm sorry, I'm just too busy."

So the question is: How do you get members to volunteer their time, talents and energy? And if they've volunteered once, how do you get them to do it again?

According to research on people who are active in social and political movements, the choice to get involved is based on three factors:

1 The organization's goal has to be important to people.

2 People must believe that what they're being asked to do will realistically lead to the achievement of that goal.

3 People must believe that their participation is necessary for the action to lead to achievement of the goal.

There are no guaranteed ways to be sure these factors exist in any given situation, but there *are* some solid guidelines on the successful recruitment and retention of member-volunteers.

LISTENING

It's hard to do, but it's absolutely necessary. You must listen. Union members will take on responsibility for their own reasons, not yours. But you need to know what their reasons are. And you find out by listening to them.

In fact, it pays to use the 80/20 Rule. Spend no more than 20 percent of your time talking, and at least 80 percent of your time listening. Such a conversation can take as little as ten minutes at a break, at lunch, or before or after work.

For example, you listen to someone and find out that they care a lot about a safety issue. If this is something important to the union, you might ask them to investigate. You're matching a need of the union with something the member cares about.

If someone is new at work and is interested in meeting others, you might put him or her in charge of a survey that needs to be done. But you will never know what people care about unless you listen to them—face to face.

Asking people what they care about is like hanging out with a purpose. Ask open-ended questions—questions that cannot be answered just yes or no. For example: "How do you like working here? What do you think about this place? What do you think is not so good?" Pay attention and don't interrupt. Hear them out. If they say something, but you think more is there, say, "Could you tell me a little more about what you mean?"

PAYOFFS

It's important for you to learn what the payoffs are for volunteering. What are the needs that motivate members to give their time to union activities? For some people it is a need to build or maintain a sense of self-esteem, to show off their creativity or receive recognition for their contribution. For others, the desire to volunteer is rooted in a need for connection, a need to be with and accepted by other people who share common values. And for still other people it may be a belief that by volunteering, they are helping to ensure their job security or improve their wages and benefits. Whatever the need, it is important to make sure you understand it and be sure it is satisfied.

ASKING FOR HELP

The first step in recruiting volunteers is to ask for help. To be effective, recruitment needs to be personal—done face-to-face and one-on-one. And then, remember the following three points:

1 ASK PEOPLE TO DO SMALL, SPECIFIC, MANAGEABLE TASKS WITH DEFINITE END POINTS. If a steward asked a member to help out by trying to get all her friends to come to the next union meeting, would she be likely to do it? Probably not—the task is too big and too vague and she wouldn't know where to start. It's better to ask the member to contact five people over the next two days and bring them to the meeting. Or, ask her to provide the names of the five people for the steward to contact. She'd be much more likely to accept the assignment. Why? Because:

☞ The member doesn't have to spend any time thinking about the task or making decisions about who to approach; you've already made the job simple and clear.

☞ The task you're asking the member to undertake is relatively small and easy.

☞ The member will know when she's done.

That last reason is fairly important. People need the sense of accomplishment that comes from finishing a task, no matter how small it is. Ideally, the task should have a number attached to it so people can measure their progress.

If you give members specific numbers of people to contact, for example, they'll know when they're halfway done—and how much remains. They'll know when they're done. The experience has been pleasurable in that way. They've accomplished something, and may want to do it again.

2 IF AT ALL POSSIBLE, GIVE PEOPLE A CHOICE OF TASKS. The person who hates calling members on the phone may not mind stuffing envelopes. The person who feels uncomfortable handing out leaflets may be great at writing a story for the newsletter. One person may want to be involved in decision-making and planning the event, another may just want to be told what to do.

3 REWARD PEOPLE. Maybe it sounds crude, but the fact is most people like to get paid for what they do, even volunteers. However, the payment may be the sense of pride from doing the right thing. For some, the payment could be public recognition and a thank-you at a union meeting. Or getting their picture in the union newsletter. Or a free union jacket.

What constitutes a reward may vary from person to person, but nobody likes to be just used and tossed aside. Instead of a perfunctory thank you to everyone who helped, spend some time thanking people individually. Everyone wants to get something for their efforts.

Be specific. Tell each member how his or her work is contributing to the overall goal. People work harder if they understand *how* they're helping, and that other people are depending on them for the success of the project. Sharing the knowledge about how their efforts will help the union and, in turn, help themselves is a powerful tool in motivating volunteers.

SOME RECRUITMENT SUGGESTIONS

☛ If you're asking a member to show up for the first time, or to do a task that's unfamiliar, you need to be present at that activity yourself. Your presence allows the volunteer to see someone familiar and allows you to demonstrate the kinds of behaviors you want the others to follow.

☛ Encourage member-volunteers to ask questions of you. This is especially important if what they are being asked to do is new or unfamiliar to them. Knowing that they can ask questions offers them reassurance and builds their confidence.

☛ If you think it will help, don't hesitate to tell the member who else will be helping with the project. For some people it is the social relationships that inspire their desire to volunteer their time and talent.

☛ Have confidence in your ability to recruit volunteers. Be persuasive and turn maybe into a definite commitment. Don't take a no answer without asking for a reason. And if you get a firm no, don't take it personally; let the volunteer know that you will miss his help and that you will be asking for help again.

☛ Provide members with the training and necessary tools to successfully accomplish the task. Nothing succeeds like success, and if you don't provide the right training or tools you are setting yourself up for a one-time-only volunteer.

☛ Keep in touch with the member as the task moves toward completion. Check to see how it is progressing. This helps you find problems as they appear and allows you to recognize the member's contributions as they occur. It also lets the member know that you will be holding her accountable for her work.

☞ Allow the member-volunteers to develop a sense of ownership where possible. Make them part of the planning process; ask for ideas and opinions. Let them have a real voice in shaping decisions.

☞ Recognize and find ways to reward the contributions that the members make. Reinforcing good work helps people want to contribute again.

☞ And finally, keep records on the volunteers. Note which projects they worked on and how much time they contributed. Keep track of the members' skills and note any new ones that may have been acquired as a result of union projects. This way you can build a member-volunteer bank, which will come in handy the next time an important union project comes up.

STEVE MAGNUSON

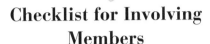

Checklist for Involving Members

☞ Appeal to their self-interest.

☞ Appeal for support of a larger cause.

☞ Remind potential volunteers of skills or experience they have to contribute.

☞ Be honest about the work involved.

☞ Recruit people from all subgroups.

☞ Start with specific, easy tasks, then gradually encourage greater involvement.

☞ Match volunteers to tasks based on their skills, interest and time.

☞ Provide training for volunteers.

☞ Teach people how to get others to share the work.

☞ Make it fun to participate.

☞ Point out every small victory to prove that involvement pays off.

☞ Arrange recognition for work that volunteers do.

☞ Check on people to see if they need help.

☞ Hold people accountable, and shift them to another assignment if the task isn't getting done.

CREATING UNIONISTS, NOT JUST MEMBERS

If members don't feel any loyalty or commitment to your union it isn't necessarily because labor history is not being taught in the schools or because the media is biased against us. It may be because the union became a closed club that stopped making new people feel welcome.

People who've gone through organizing drives know why unions are formed. People who grew up in a family where somebody was a union member also know what unions are about and what they do. But for the average person starting work on a new job in a unionized workplace, chances are that all they know about unions is what they read in the paper or see on TV.

It isn't a new member's responsibility to educate himself about unions. It's *our* responsibility.

There are several ways the union can orient the new member:

☞ Negotiate for time in the employer's orientation session.

☞ Invite (or require) new members to attend a special union meeting where an orientation takes place.

☞ Hold a "Lunch and Learn" at the workplace—a half-hour orientation session. Ask the employer if you can use a meeting room. Order pizza for everyone.

☛ Do an informational one-on-one with the new worker.

ORIENTATION MEETINGS

If you have a large enough group to justify holding an orientation meeting, whether it's at the workplace, the union hall or elsewhere, here are some things to keep in mind: Try to get some back-and-forth discussion going. Allow time for questions. Ask questions of the new workers. Try to break up the meeting so it's not just you talking at them the whole time.

If this feels uncomfortable, though, don't force it. Most of them may not know enough yet to have questions. In fact, you may want to think about holding some kind of follow-up orientation after people have been on the job six months or so, when they've had some experience.

Think about *who* should do the orientation. In a more diverse workforce, you want people who are representing the union to mirror that workforce. Try to get a real cross-section of members involved in the orientation, including women, people of different races and younger members, so new members from those groups feel it's their organization too.

Talk about what's interesting to the new workers. Don't try to go over every benefit in the contract. They won't remember the details anyway.

New employees, especially younger ones, are primarily interested in pay and time off. So, talk about one or two of the contract provisions that relate to those issues.

Be sure to spend some time talking about the grievance procedure. It's one of the biggest differences between a union and a nonunion workplace and most new employees will be unfamiliar with the idea. You'll make your work as steward a lot easier down the road if you spend some time up front educating new members about what constitutes a grievance and how the grievance process works.

Above all, don't let those who are anti-union get under your skin. Don't argue. If someone makes negative comments—and they will—be positive about the union and try to find common ground. Don't make them feel defensive or you'll never win them over. Always be personable, polite and understanding, even if deep down inside you're tempted to toss them out the nearest window. Remember, they don't yet know about the union. Your job is to give them the facts. Be patient. People will come around in their own time; your job is to help them along.

Research has shown that personal contact with the union during the first few months of employment is strongly related to whether the member feels loyal to the union over the long term. So, the effort you make today will pay the union back for many years to come.

ONE-ON-ONE ORIENTATION

The Communications Workers of America negotiated a provision in their contract with AT&T that allows stewards a half-hour one-on-one with each new employee. Stewards don't spend that time just describing the union, however. Instead, they spend the first ten minutes talking to the new member in a personal way about their interests and their background.

The information a steward gives a new worker isn't necessarily the most important part of the initial meeting, anyway. What the new worker is likely to remember is whether or not they felt comfortable with you, whether they liked you, whether they

thought you were really interested in them or if you were just trying to sell them something. That's going to be their first impression of the union.

If you're not able to get the employer to give you one-on-one time during working hours, take the new person out to lunch or introduce yourself on break. They're probably feeling a little lost anyway; they don't know anybody. They'll remember if the first person who made an effort to be nice to them was from the union.

THE RIGHT-TO-WORK CHALLENGE

As challenging as it can be to serve as a steward, nowhere is the challenge greater than in a right-to-work state or in an open shop. There, everybody in a workplace covered by a union contract enjoys all the benefits the union can wrest from management, but workers are not required to belong to the union and pay their fair share of the costs involved in keeping it running.

It can be frustrating, but it's not impossible to build a strong union. It's done all the time, by dedicated unionists who seize opportunities whenever they can.

For example, union membership at a Nashville hospital was low. Every nonmember had something they didn't like about the union or some excuse not to join: in Tennessee, one of the nation's twenty-one right-to-work states, there's no such thing as automatic union membership.

Then a real organizing issue reared its head: just two weeks before Christmas, hospital management revised the schedule and told hundreds of employees they'd have to work on the holiday.

The union saw a solid opportunity to organize among the free riders, and grabbed it. The union asked every employee—members and nonmembers—to attend a mass meeting in the cafeteria to confront the administrator. The nonmembers were mad enough over the schedule change to respond, and they got a real taste of what unity can do when the work schedules were switched back. By the time the union was through, membership had jumped by nearly 20 percent.

There's no magic to recruiting members into your union when membership is voluntary. The basics are to give potential members a good reason to get involved; have a plan that can be carried out; and ask the workers, directly, to join.

A GOOD REASON TO GET INVOLVED

People join organizations when they believe they will be better off for it. If they can't see any direct gain, they figure, why pay dues?

Let them see the gain, or potential for gain. Take action on issues. Make your members—and the free riders—feel like a part of something greater. The last-minute hospital schedule change in Nashville affected workers directly: it was about the opportunity to spend time with families and about respect for employees and their own lives.

HAVE A PLAN

Develop issue campaigns for members to get involved in, and don't wait until contract time approaches. Pick a problem that bothers a large group of the workers represented by the union and figure out who has the ability to change it. Plot out a series of steps to force change.

Start with smaller issues that may be easier to solve (for example, better furniture in the employee break room) than a big one, like eliminating all favoritism.

Both the steward and the union should have lists of each member and nonmember in every work area. Use a rating system to track each employee, such as: 1—active union member, 2—inactive union member, 3—neutral nonmember, 4—somewhat anti-union nonmember, 5—very anti-union nonmember.

Hold rallies and demonstrations to push your issue. Circulate petitions, send postcards, wear armbands and T-shirts, use street theater. If you have 5 to 10 percent of your members actively participating in union-sponsored actions, you'll have an impact.

The hospital workers in Nashville didn't start by asking nonmembers to join the union: they asked them to help roll back a management decision that made a lot of lives miserable, member and non-member alike. Even the most skeptical workers were willing to try to do something about the schedule change.

Don't let your anger and resentment get in the way. Listen carefully to what the individual nonmember says. Don't make assumptions. Try and see the union through their eyes. Do they have a real fear of retaliation? Have they had a bad experience with the union in the past? Is there a personal or financial problem? What is their self-interest? What contribution could they make to the union?

ASK THEM DIRECTLY TO JOIN

In survey after survey, union members in open shops say they joined because someone they knew approached them. And nonmembers say the leading reason they don't join is because no one ever directly asks them to. No matter how effective your plan may be, it won't accomplish your objective—getting nonmembers to join up—unless you ask them directly, one-on-one, to join.

USING PRESSURE TO SETTLE GRIEVANCES

What ultimately settles grievances? More often than not, it hinges on the union's ability to pressure management to settle.

When managers look at the steward and the grievant across the table at a grievance meeting, they must clearly understand that they are dealing with more than just two people. They are dealing with the entire union. Management must also go to the grievance meeting feeling some immediacy so they don't drag the grievance out through all the steps.

The steward's role is to orchestrate this pressure on management. It means that a steward must think and act like an organizer rather than getting caught up in the lawyer-client scene that so often surrounds the grievance procedure.

How the steward orchestrates pressure, and the amount of pressure needed, will differ from workplace to workplace. It will also differ with the seriousness of the grievance issue.

In determining the amount of pressure necessary to settle the grievance, the steward should brainstorm these questions with the grievant and other members:

- How serious is this kind of grievance? Some incidents actually threaten worker well-being: safety and health violations, sexual harassment, discrimination, suspensions and firings. Others are more of the nuisance variety: failure to pay overtime, scheduling by seniority, minor forms of discipline. While every legitimate grievance requires the steward's attention, often the less serious ones can be settled quickly through informal dealings with the supervisor.
- How widespread is this kind of grievance? An incident that affects a number of workers will generate more pressure from the workers themselves. A pattern of isolated incidents against individuals may demonstrate that management is cracking down and establishing a pattern to undermine the contract.
- What has management's response

been toward this incident? The steward should expect that management will initially deny guilt. But if the denial is coupled with harshness or arrogance, you'll want to crank up the pressure machine.

Orchestrating pressure should be a fun and creative activity for the steward and his co-workers. It opens up the grievance procedure and allows workers to direct their energy to solving the problem, not waiting for something to happen or someone to solve it for them. Pressure activities can be designed so that workers begin with low-risk, minimum-time-commitment steps (signing a group petition) and build up so that they become comfortable with higher-risk, more time-consuming activities (job action).

Stewards should work with their union officials on orchestrating the appropriate pressure activities. Here are some examples.

SUBTLE PRESSURE

- Talking it up in the workplace. Workers discuss the case among themselves, within earshot of supervisors.
- Education. The general issue of the grievance—insubordination, sexual harassment or whatever—is the sub-

ject for lunchtime or break meetings; flyers appear around the workplace announcing it.

- Publicity. Bulletin board notices (probably more faithfully read by supervisors than workers), flyers, articles in workplace newsletters appear about the issue involved in the grievance.

- Workers make sure the grievance is known about by the supervisor's supervisor, other supervisors and up the chain of command. This can be as simple as workers in different departments making casual comments all on the same day to their supervisors, such as, "The food service supervisor really treats his workers like dirt."

- Workers from other departments sign the bottom of the grievance to show support.

DIRECT PRESSURE

- Workers—led by the steward—ask for a group meeting with management about the grievance issue. Even if the meeting is denied, the union makes the point that people know and are concerned.

- Workers wear a button, sticker or armband to express their solidarity behind the union's grievance.

- Workers sign a petition calling for swift and rightful resolution of the grievance and present it in a group to key management people.

- Workers alert the clients, customers and/or the outside public about the grievance issue through informational leafleting, rallies and use of the media.

Experienced stewards find that involving workers is a much more satisfying way of handling grievances. They also report that grievance wins are far more fulfilling than solving the problem alone with the individual grievant. And even grievance losses serve to unite workers more around blaming management—rather than the union steward—for the loss.

HELPING WIN BETTER CONTRACTS

It's a lot harder to get a fair contract now than it was thirty years ago. In the private sector today, management backs up its demands by threatening to move jobs out of the area or even out of the country. In the public sector, management threatens to turn jobs over to private contractors.

More and more unions are responding to these tactics by bringing heavier weapons into their bargaining arsenals. One of these is the increased involvement of stewards and the entire membership in setting and achieving bargaining goals.

There's a lot that stewards and members can do. Situations and styles vary union by union and employer by employer, but here are some tactics to consider to increase your union's strength at the bargaining table.

KEEP ACCURATE RECORDS

The bargaining cycle is continuous. After a contract is won, you should immediately begin collecting data on contract violations and issues for the next round of bargaining. The more ammunition your negotiators have, the better they can fight the war.

SURVEY THE MEMBERSHIP

If the local leadership decides to develop a survey on bargaining goals and priorities, stewards can go to each member in their department and fill out a short survey, talking to each member one-on-one.

DEVELOP A COMMUNICATIONS NETWORK

If you're called on to update your co-workers on progress in bargaining, you may find yourself speaking with members individually, leafletting or setting up phone trees. You may want to recruit active members to help with some of the chores.

HELP THE LEADERSHIP ORGANIZE ACTIVITIES

Workplace actions or demonstrations are often necessary to pressure management to agree or to show that the membership is united around bargaining goals. Pressure tactics can range from all members wearing a button or T-shirt with the theme of the campaign to noontime rallies at the offices of management.

SERVE ON CONTRACT CAMPAIGN COMMITTEES

Many unions set up a variety of contract campaign committees. These committees can publicize the union's cause; organize community support; contact other unions for mutual support; recruit politicians, religious leaders and others to help; and organize social events to boost morale or raise funds.

SPOT LEGAL OR REGULATORY PROBLEMS

Stewards can involve the members in tracking health and safety problems, environmental or regulatory violations, or mismanagement. Documenting management failings in these areas can be a huge help. Not only can they help your bargainers by putting some valuable chips on the table in front of them, but they're a great way to build activism and unity.

HELP BUILD AND MAINTAIN SOLIDARITY

Help get the members to attend meetings or rallies about the contract, or give them that button or T-shirt and remind them to wear it. Everyone needs to get involved and stay involved at a level that's comfortable for them. Mutual support and encouragement is vital.

Times have changed. Union members need to be more organized than ever before to achieve success at the bargaining table. An educated, active, united membership is the key to obtaining good contracts. Stewards can work with local and international union leadership to achieve the goal.

RALLYING THE TROOPS WITH LAUGHTER AND SONG

We do what we want to do
Say what we want to say
Spend what we want to spend
Pay what we want to pay . . .

This musical rap, done to the theme song from *The Addams Family*, was sung by the "boss" in a skit performed at a union conference. The boss was addressing his employees as "one big happy family," which led one worker to remark, "His idea of a happy family is the Addams family!"

Sounds like fun. But what does it have to do with the workplace problems faced by shop stewards? More than you might think.

Satirical skits, affirms Julie McCall, a Washington, D.C., hospital worker and long-time union activist, are a great tool for anticipating management strategies and helping workers gain the confidence to challenge injustices on the job. It can be very empowering to have a chance to portray a supervisor who has been on your back for years and to make him or her look ridiculous!

If you're looking for ways to increase membership involvement and generate some enthusiasm at meetings, consider trying a skit with a game show format, such as, *Your Job's in Jeopardy*, starring Pat Payback. You can create your own management team with characters, such as Phil R. Banks or Bozo Boss. The audience becomes the union team.

The management team always answers the questions wrong, of course, and the union gives the correct answers and wins more new members.

You can even add commercials: the Energizer Bunny can appear, for example, and announce, "The union keeps growing and growing and growing."

With a little imagination, you can come up with a skit to fit just about any situation.

One group was holding an event where members brought their children, and the kids wanted to participate. They came up with a skit, *The Teenage Mutant Union Turtle*, complete with a *Turtle Power* rap song. The Turtles had to go up against RamBoss, whose costume included balloon "muscles" under his shirtsleeves. The kids defeated him by popping his muscles.

Another example: "I know just the company for us. They'll save us money and

they'll suck the blood out of the union. Let me introduce . . . *CONTRACTULA!*" So entered union-buster "Contractula" in a skit written and performed by a group of union stewards and officers from the American Federation of Teachers. They wanted to demonstrate the impact of contracting out union jobs to nonunion companies. By the time Contractula and his vampire chorus had finished their "Union Busters" rap (to the tune of "Ghost Busters"), there wasn't a member in the room who didn't understand the issue—or anyone who would forget about it any time soon!

One important function of a union steward is helping members understand their contract, McCall stresses. Finding creative ways to present your material is often key to generating interest and excitement. There are few union events that couldn't benefit from an injection of pizzazz.

SKITS THAT ARE HITS

Remember these principles when creating and casting a skit:

1 **Base your skit on an experience that is common to your audience.** The supervisors who are the most notoriously unfair can be turned into characters like Bosszilla, Boss Hogg or RamBoss.

2 **Exaggerate!** Take an issue or situation that's outrageous to begin with and carry it to the extreme. In a 1980s skit about the Eastern Airlines strike, for example, airline owners Frank Lorenzo, Donald Trump and Carl Icahn were portrayed in a poker game in which the stakes were airline routes, airport gates, passengers and employees.

3 **Put forth some type of solution or action the union is taking.** In one production "BatRep" and "Rockin' Robin" arrived on the scene (complete with taped theme songs) to help union members organize to solve their problems.

4 **You don't need fancy props and costumes.** You can make signs to identify characters or scenes, or make your action revolve around one central prop. One group drew a computer screen on a large cardboard box, put the box on someone's head, and came up with a talking computer that had some great dialogue with the computer operators.

5 **Make it easy for people to participate.** Write out the script and let players read their lines if they're not comfortable memorizing their parts. The key is to have fun.

WORDS AND MUSIC

Now that you're on a roll, why not come up with a song to go with your skit? The easiest way to do this is to write new words to a tune that everyone already knows. Christmas carols, children's songs, gospel tunes, popular songs . . . anything goes. But pick a song and musical that your particular membership can identify with.

If you want to use current hit songs and don't have musicians available, find a record store that sells 12-inch singles or extended mix dance records and tapes. These usually contain one version of the song with instruments alone. You can write your own words and then pop in a tape and sing along.

There is also a company that sells instrumental versions of popular songs on tapes. They can be lots of fun to sing along with after you rewrite the words. For instance, "Stand By Me" can be changed to "My Union Stands By Me" or "My Steward Stands By Me," with a verse like the following:

When the boss calls to say
I have to work on Saturday
And a grievance form is what I really
   need
I'm not up-tight at all
Cause I'll just give my steward a call
Yes, I know that my steward stands by me

Chorus
Oh brothers, sisters
Stand by me, oh stand by me
I know that my steward stands by me

For a sample tape catalogue you can write to Pocketsongs, 50 Executive Blvd., Elmsford NY 10523-1325, or call 1-800-NOW SING. For musical ideas you can put to work in your own situation contact the Labor Heritage Foundation, an organization of labor musicians, artists and writers, at 815 16th St. NW, Washington, DC 20006. Phone: 202-842-7880.

Don't forget to think about holiday music, too. During the big Pittston Coal strike, the miners had their own holiday songbook called, "Camo-Carols" with parodies such as, "I'm Dreaming of a Fair Contract" and "Arrest Those Union Gentlemen" (to the tune of "God Rest Ye Merry Gentlemen"). The possibilities are endless.

A helpful tool for prospective songwriters is a rhyming dictionary. (You can buy a pocket edition for a few dollars.) This great little book will give you lists of words that rhyme with a particular word or sound. So you can make a vocabulary list of names of bosses, issues, job terminology and so on, then use the rhyming dictionary to find words that rhyme with the words on your list. After that you'll probably find that your song will fall into place pretty quickly.

Don't be afraid to use your imagination—you'll be surprised at how easily you can turn what could have been a rather dull union event into an exciting experience when you say it in a song or skit.

So, the next time you have a stewards' meeting coming up, try doing what Julie McCall and other activists have been doing, successfully, for years: organize a group to do a song or a skit and see what a difference it makes in your event. When you deal with serious issues in creative ways, you're guaranteed to keep your members coming back for more.

YES, IT WORKS!

Principles and hints and tactics are fine, but there's nothing like seeing a few examples of how mobilization can work. The following are real case studies—some names and places have been changed—of winning mobilization efforts.

BLOWING THE WHISTLE ON CONTRACT VIOLATIONS

"Hello, Dad—it's Jess. I've got a problem with the foreman at the shop that won't go away and I figured you could talk me through it. I'm on my way over."

When things got real tough for Jesse Kline, union steward at AMCO Tool and Dye, he could always rely on his father for good advice. After all, back in the '50s Ron Kline helped organize the union at the company, and he had served ten years as president. With grudging respect, the plant manager still says the happiest day in his life was the day Ron Kline retired.

Jesse explained the problem to his dad. Over the past year he had filed twelve grievances against the same foreman on the same issue: the foreman would operate the forklift any time he saw fit. This was a clear violation of Article 6 of the union's contract, which stated, ". . . and management will not perform any bargaining unit work, including the operation of warehouse vehicles such as forklifts, except in times of severe emergencies." Even after two separate arbitrators ruled in the union's favor, the company was still allowing the foreman to operate the forklift.

Jesse explained to his father that the members were grumbling about the union and asking tough questions. What was the purpose of their thirteen-week strike two winters ago if management ignored the contract anyway? What good is it to take your problems to the shop steward when management simply ignores the contract?

With negotiations on a new agreement deadlocked, the forklift issue was dividing the workers from the union leadership. Management knew the workers would be reluctant to strike for a contract that they felt the union couldn't enforce.

"Dad, I don't know what to do. Management is creating the problem but our members are blaming me and the union. It's playing right into the hands of the company."

Ron Kline held back a smile in the confident manner all fathers use when their kids come to them for the simple answers to seemingly impossible problems. He gave two pieces of advice.

First, he pointed to Article 6 in Jesse's dog-eared copy of the contract and with a twinkle in his eye he said to his son, "This certainly seems like a severe emergency to me."

Then, in a serious tone, the veteran of many labor battles told the frustrated steward, "It's not the grievances, son, it's the numbers that count."

The next day at AMCO, with a hurricane-force blast, Mary Victor blew a metal whistle that her shop steward had given her that morning. Instantly, blowing their own whistles, the rest of the workers stopped what they were doing and rushed to Mary's work area. When Jesse made his way to the center of the whistling crowd, there sat the foreman, on an idling forklift, stunned.

"Where's the flood, or is it a fire?" Jesse asked the foreman.

"What's going on here? There's no flood or fire," replied the puzzled and confused foreman, obviously shaken by the shrill mass that surrounded him.

"There's gotta be *some* emergency," retorted the steward, "because the contract says management can only operate forklifts during severe emergencies. So where's the fire, boss?"

The foreman dismounted and cursed his way through the whistling crowd. As the glass door to his office closed behind him the union members cheered. Jesse Kline gave them the thumbs-up sign and as he walked to the back of the warehouse he thought to himself, "Dad was right, it's numbers that count."

The union members had to pull two more "emergency alerts" that week but after that the foreman left the forklift alone. By mobilizing his members and spending $20 on whistles Jesse Kline had won in a week what $6000 in arbitration costs and one year of grievances couldn't solve.

Shop stewards everywhere can tell stories about the ways management delays and manipulates the grievance procedure to undermine the union. By activating his members, Jesse Kline was able to derail management's attempt to isolate the shop steward and weaken the union.

WRITING UP THE BOSS

Too often shop stewards are saddled with supervisors who believe their role in life is to turn the workplace into a branch of the Marine Corps.

You know the type: they go strictly by the book even when the book is wrong. They lie in wait for the slightest error and fan disciplinary slips in the faces of unsuspecting workers. They constantly order employees to perform functions clearly prohibited by the contract. Workers who refuse to obey now and grieve later are charged with the serious offense of insubordination. And just try to ask these supervisors for some help. That's not their job—they're here to let us know when we screw up.

Some unions have devised ways to mobilize their members to give these gung ho supervisors a taste of their own medicine. For example, the California Nurses Association (CNA) developed a special form entitled Assignment Despite Objection (ADO). An ADO is a discipline slip for *supervisors* and is filled out by any union member who feels she or he has been given an assignment that is unsafe or may place a patient in jeopardy.

The form has a section for the name of the offending supervisor and sections for information on patient/nurse ratios, forced overtime and other hazardous situations.

The ADO is printed in quadruplicate with one copy going to the supervisor, one copy going to the nurse, another copy going to CNA, and the final copy going to the hospital's Professional Performance Committee.

Another variation of the writing-up-the-boss strategy comes from Service Employees International Union Local 535 in Los Angeles. The union encourages its members—also nurses—to turn in annual evaluations on their supervisors. Nurses give their supervisors from zero to four points in twenty-three categories ranging from "helping out with patient care" to "dresses appropriately." The results are tallied for each supervisor and published for the entire hospital staff to see.

The SEIU annual evaluations and CNA's supervisor discipline forms demonstrate how unions can activate their members to win results. One CNA organizer explained: "Writing up management allows us to involve our members in efforts to improve working conditions and health care for our patients. We are putting supervisors on notice that the union will hold them publicly accountable when they mistreat employees."

LET'S DO LUNCH

Priscilla Gordon had been the president of Food Workers Local 99 at the New

England Cod & Bean Co. just prior to Ron Pengrove. Gordon had resigned the office to become the company's personnel director. Pengrove knew that despite Gordon's good record as union president, it was just a matter of time before she would show which side she was now on.

That day came when a senior worker complained to Pengrove that personnel wouldn't let him take a promotion exam for an opening in the maintenance department. Pengrove went to Gordon and informed her that this was a violation of the contract. Gordon's response was that she didn't care what the contract said: "Everyone knows this guy will never pass the exam, so why waste the time. If you don't like my decision, go spend the union's money and arbitrate it."

This put Pengrove in a difficult spot. He didn't like the idea of letting arbitrators make decisions on things that the contract already guaranteed to the union. Nor did he want Gordon getting into the habit of stonewalling every union grievance.

On the other hand, if he went over Gordon's head and approached the plant manager, the manager would ask Gordon's advice and Gordon would assure him that she knows the members' feelings—she used to be local union president, after all—and they would never get upset over the issue.

The manager, Pengrove reasoned, would most likely believe Gordon.

Thinking about how to handle the problem, Pengrove remembered that once, when Gordon was union president, the executive board had been discussing the issue of membership apathy and low attendance at union meetings. Pengrove had suggested that the union hold informal monthly meetings with members in the lunchroom during meals and breaks. By inviting everyone in the lunchroom to participate, the union would be giving out information and getting important feedback from everyone, not just the same crowd that regularly attended union meetings.

The idea had never gotten off the ground: Gordon and the others had decided against the lunchroom idea for fear it would give people another reason not to attend the regular meetings, and because the members wouldn't want their regular lunch routines interrupted.

Pengrove decided to give it a try. For the next two Wednesdays Ron Pengrove and the Local 99 stewards held lunch meetings about the company's new policy of forcing everything to arbitration and ignoring the promotion clause of the contract.

The first lunch meeting attracted a curious crowd of 150 members.

The second lunch meeting attracted a crowd of 250—who decided to picket outside the company for the last fifteen minutes of their lunch break.

Lo and behold, Priscilla Gordon changed her mind and allowed the grievant to take the exam. Ron Pengrove had discovered another reason to have lunch meetings: management couldn't stomach it.

MAKING SYMBOLISM WORK FOR YOU

Symbols play a powerful role in American life. We're proud of the flag, we wear green on St. Patrick's Day, the scales of justice adorn the front of many local courthouses. Likewise, when union stewards and activists develop ways to blend in symbols with grassroots mobilization techniques, bold management assaults can be turned into hasty retreats.

Certain symbols evoke strong emotional responses. By enlisting these symbols, unions find it easier to generate more enthusiasm and greater participation from members, and more sympathy from the public.

For example, when the president of United Press International demanded that union reporters give up Independence Day, Labor Day and Christmas as paid holidays the reporters greeted him with a chorus of "Jingle Bells" every time he walked into the

newsroom. After he verbally reprimanded one of the louder union carolers, he was flooded daily with anonymous Christmas cards—in the month of June.

Similarly, the Service Employees International Union in Denver was fighting attempts by a local bank to use nonunion janitorial contractors. The union janitors decided to summon one of the most powerful symbols of the Christmas spirit—Santa Claus. Union janitors converged on the bank lobby (one dressed in a Santa suit) to perform their services for free. The nation's first clean-in didn't go over big with bank management: they had the jolly janitors escorted out by police. The story on TV news that evening was a twist on another symbol of Christmas—Charles Dickens' *A Christmas Carol*. The bank was portrayed as a greedy Ebenezer Scrooge and the plight of the janitors was compared to that of Tiny Tim. Add to this the bold images of Santa Claus in the grasp of police and you begin to understand why bank management had a sudden change of heart and decided to use a union cleaning service.

Christmas isn't the only holiday that symbolically lends itself to rank-and-file mobilization. Nursing home workers have successfully planned events around Mother's Day, many a pain-in-the-butt boss has been honored with a golden turkey award on Thanksgiving, and it can set off fireworks when workers demand a Workplace Bill of Rights on Independence Day.

Three common threads run through all these events: the members' opportunity to creatively confront the employer, the employer's total vulnerability to such tactics, and the strong appeal to the public's sense of morality.

The next time you need to make a point by activating the members, keep in mind the extra energy an appropriate symbol will add to your fight.

CALLING ON AT&T

The *American Heritage Dictionary's* second definition of the word *mobilize* is "to assemble, prepare or put into operation for war or similar emergency." The Communications Workers of America had such an emergency when one of their contracts with AT&T expired. But they were ready. They had initiated what they called Mobilization CWA, where stewards and other specially trained mobilizers were assigned to get the 120,000 AT&T workers involved in a campaign for a better contract.

Like the dictionary definition, Mobilization CWA also had three elements: organize, educate and act. CWA first organized a structure in which they identified and trained one steward or mobilizer for every ten to twenty workers.

Next, they educated the members about the key issues in negotiations—job security, a decent standard of living and maintenance of health care coverage—by talking to each worker one-on-one.

Finally, CWA members acted by engaging themselves in several nationwide shop and office floor actions.

These actions started slow and built in intensity as the contract expiration date approached. First, tens of thousands of postcards were collected and sent to AT&T's chairman. Next, at every AT&T worksite in the country, CWA members wore red shirts on Thursdays. On another occasion, all AT&T office workers and operators stood up at their work stations at the same time because they were participating in Take a Stand Day. On another day, tens of thousands of AT&T workers showed up to work wearing bloody bandages, walking on crutches and riding wheelchairs to protest management's efforts to roll back health care coverage.

The final straw for management came when the company learned that millions of wallet-size cards had been printed explaining how consumers could bypass AT&T operators to use competing long distance companies. Rumor had it that CWA was going to use its mobilization network to distribute these cards nationwide to family members and other trade union members.

The new contract was signed without a strike—and without concessions.

A COOL RECEPTION

A group of Colorado office workers were having a difficult time convincing the office manager that their building had adequate heat.

It was never determined whether management was trying to reduce energy costs at the expense of worker health, or just trying to be sadistic. One thing was sure: the members of the union knew that if they waited until all the steps in the grievance

procedure were exhausted, it would be summer before they got any heat.

Mary, the union steward, had a brilliant strategy for a solidarity action. Over the weekend, the union's solidarity committee was busy calling the entire workforce at home. On Monday morning, when the office manager entered the building—late as usual—he was shocked to see all fifty union members wearing overcoats, mufflers and mittens at their typing stations.

When he demanded an explanation, Mary told him that this was necessary to protect worker health and safety. The manager decided it was cooler to stoke up the furnace than to feel the heat from a united workforce.

7 DEALING WITH DIFFICULT PEOPLE

Grievance-handling and union-building work is never easy. What can make it even harder is the human element, like when you have a supervisor who feels his manhood is on the line every minute of the workday, or a co-worker who finds fault with everything the union does.

The effective steward knows that understanding the union contract is only half the battle. A good chunk of the other half is knowing how to deal with the people around you. In this chapter we offer some suggestions, beginning with problems stewards can encounter within their own ranks, and moving on to typical issues and attitudes presented to stewards by management.

THE STEWARD AS PSYCHOLOGIST

The whiner. The malcontent. The habitually lazy (or late or absent) worker. The loose cannon. The apathetic. The critic. The snitch.

Stewards often report that the most challenging part of their job—and the most frustrating—is dealing with difficult workers. It's also time-consuming, burning up valuable hours that stewards would rather use working on grievances or organizing around important workplace issues.

Why deal with these people at all? Won't ignoring their irritating behavior make it go away? Unfortunately not. Such people have a way of infecting those around them, even if others recognize them as difficult. At best, difficult people dampen morale; at worst, they get others to think and act as they do. It's best to confront the problem directly.

How can you, the steward, deal with difficult people and keep your sanity?

Several principles are useful to keep in mind when handling difficult personalities. People are cooperative—unless they are hurting in some way. Reaching for the person underneath the hurt with welcoming and nonjudgmental words and tones can often defuse the situation. This also means treating the person with complete respect and avoiding putting him or her down. Notice what increases the hostility and defensiveness and what decreases it.

Another point to keep in mind is you cannot effectively handle a difficult interaction if *both* people are being difficult. If your buttons have been pushed by this person, it is usually better to deal with that elsewhere (for example, talk with someone else, preferably someone outside your workplace, about what's hard about dealing with that person).

Lastly, many abrasive or uncooperative behaviors and attitudes are habits people have learned from the past to deal with their surroundings. They're not necessarily well-thought-out strategies. There is a difference between the person and the patterns they are stuck in. Assisting them to work through these ineffective habits will not only be helpful for the person but will also unleash a much more effective union supporter.

Here are some techniques that are useful for dealing with a variety of problem causers.

ACTIVELY LISTENING

Realize that some people are difficult because they feel no one has ever completely heard them out. Give the worker a chance to vent, but feel free to set a time limit. For example, "LaShawna, I've heard you say some negative things about the union. Let's sit together at lunch for twenty minutes and you tell me what's going on."

As you listen, try to figure out the reason for the behavior. Ask probing questions. "Why do you feel that way?" Send up trial balloons to narrow the possible sources. "So you're angry with the union because it lost a grievance for you three years ago?"

Actively listening means questioning and challenging. You need to be more than just a sounding board, because you want to come out of this encounter understanding why the worker acts this way.

DESCRIBING THE SITUATION TO THE WORKER

Often an effective way to confront the person about his or her behavior is to describe calmly what you see the person doing, how you feel about it and the effect you think it has.

"Mary Beth, I hear you tell new employees that our union is no good. I don't think that's a fair picture of the union and it dampens the interest people might have for participating and improving conditions here at work."

Notice that you don't label the person as *bad* for her behavior. This lessens the opportunity for an angry backlash. (Consider how you'd alienate Mary Beth if you'd said, "Mary Beth, you're stupid for telling new employees the union's no good.")

It gives the person a chance to consider her behavior in a new light—how it makes others feel. Once someone realizes that, she may think twice before doing it again.

IDENTIFYING THE PROBLEM AS A DILEMMA

Articulate the interests on both sides and enlist help in trying to work together on an acceptable solution.

For example, Yvonne consistently dominates a meeting and has difficulty letting other people get a word in edgewise.

At a break or outside the meeting, tell Yvonne, "I have a dilemma. Maybe you can help me figure it out. I know that you have a lot to say in the meeting. At the same time I'm trying to figure out how to encourage other people to speak up. What do you think are some ways we can get both things accomplished?"

ENLISTING OTHERS AS POSITIVE EXAMPLES

Show difficult people that there is a more constructive way to deal with what's bothering them. Ask other workers to tell difficult people their stories.

"Bob, Al here used to go to the boss and talk about his co-workers whenever he was upset with them, but he found a better way to deal with the situation. I'd like Al to tell you about it."

In addition to providing another avenue for action, it subtly puts peer pressure on the difficult person and reinforces the understanding that his behavior does upset others.

SHOW INTEREST AND COMPASSION

Workers in the unit may urge you to tell off the difficult person—and the temptation will be great. Remember that difficult people are often lonely and troubled. Sincere concern for them will probably work better than harsh words. Despite their behavior, they also deserve as much respect as any other union member.

Talk with them and try to get others to talk with them—even if initially it's just, "Hi, how are you doing?" People feel and act better when they feel a part of something.

The last thing to keep in mind is that you also deserve to be treated with respect and have the invaluable job you do as steward be recognized as such. With a little effort, you can teach your co-workers to think well about you and enlist the help of others to do this.

DEALING WITH CONSTANT CRITICS

The union isn't doing anything. . . . The union is meddling with everything.

The union is too cozy with management. . . . The union is too confrontational with management.

The union should stay out of politics. . . .

STEVE MAGNUSON

The union should do more politically.

You've probably heard all these complaints at one time or another. They come from the Union Critic. That's a worker who can be a member or nonmember, a one-time activist who soured on the union or someone who just never got involved.

For the union steward, the critic is your heckler, dampening morale within the unit and irritating you and others.

BUMMED OUT ON LIFE

One type of critic is the kind who's also negative about everything else in life. Such a person is an expert at making clouds appear in blue, sunny skies. While his or her negativism is annoying, it is also relatively harmless. Because complaining is his chief activity, this critic takes no direct action to undermine the union. A negative person does not attract followers, and usually is a loner.

Be realistic about what you can achieve with such a person. Give him a friendly ear, point out the positive and suggest ways for him to get involved. But don't be surprised if you don't make headway—this kind of person just needs to complain.

THE UNION'S DONE ME WRONG

One common type of critic is the person who feels the union has let him down by losing a grievance, not resolving an issue in bargaining or not going to the wall over some concern. This critic tells this tale of woe to anyone and everyone (often embellishing it each time it's told) and turns people off about the union.

Sometimes his dissatisfaction is fueled by misinformation or unrealistic expectations about what the union can reasonably accomplish. You should talk it through with him—perhaps no one really has explained how the grievance process works or what happens in bargaining. It's important that workers realize that the union can't perform miracles.

If what happened was a legitimate mistake on the part of the union, acknowledge it and shift the discussion to how you both can work together so it doesn't happen again. Emphasize that the union works best when people are involved.

"IT'S YOUR JOB, MAN"

Particularly frustrating for the steward is the critic who belittles what the union does, but offers no solutions. When asked to get involved in improving a bad situation, this critic pushes it off onto the steward because "it's the steward's job." If you're a steward who tries to do it all, you probably have several critics like this. But the more you can get people involved in the union's activities at the work site, the harder it is for this critic to continue his rap.

HANG IN THERE!

Overall, in dealing with critics:

Set a Positive Tone

It's hard for the critic to be critical when people are involved, the union does fun and interesting things, and new workers are greeted by positive union members first, not by the critics. In this environment, the critic will find no audience.

Listen to Criticism . . . Within Limits

No matter how unfounded the complaint, hear out the union critics. It indicates to them that you are concerned. More important, it indicates to others that you respect what workers think, that you are patient and that if others have a problem you'd rather they bring it to you first, not mouth off to others or to the boss. You can set the ground rules for letting critics have their say: they must stick to the issues, offer alternatives and commit to something they will do to improve the situation. You can also suggest a time limit and make it clear that you will not tolerate any verbal abuse.

Also make it clear why constant negativism about the union is bad—it can divide workers and dampen enthusiasm and involvement, and sets the stage for one sure event: management getting the upper hand.

Maintain an Even Temper

Since the steward is the union in workers' eyes, workers will dump the criticism on you. Don't take it personally. Understand their frustration is often misdirected. They are too scared to dump it on the boss, where most of it belongs, or on society's institutions, which appear faceless to them.

Keep a sense of humor and focus on the positive—those many workers who perform their jobs faithfully, pay their dues loyally and never complain about the union.

REPRESENTING THE ANTI-UNION WORKER

If you're thinking you won't represent an anti-union worker in a grievance situation, think again!

So disgusting is the task that one steward exclaimed, "I would rather clean my teenagers' bedrooms." And she had three teenagers.

It's a job that evokes strong reactions from most stewards.

The law says you have to defend these folks, period. As a result of a 1967 Supreme Court interpretation of the National Labor Relations Act, the union has an obligation to equally and in good faith represent everyone covered by the collective bargaining agreement. It's called the duty of fair representation, and it applies to members and nonmembers (in open-shop situations or right-to-work states) regardless of whether they like or dislike the union.

Almost without exception, it's the rule in the public sector as well as the private.

The duty of fair representation means that when *any* worker in your recognized bargaining unit brings a possible grievance to you, you must make a thorough investigation. If your investigation determines the complaint is indeed a grievance, you must follow all the procedures the union has established in handling grievances. If your investigation determines it is not a grievance, your reason for not filing one must be based on the merits of the case—not because the worker is an anti-union troublemaker.

"But it doesn't mean I have to give service with a smile," said one steward in a memorable one-liner.

No, you don't. But you might make this encounter with the anti-union worker an opportunity to change his or her mind. Or, at the very least, defuse the impact of her anti-unionism on the rest of the people in the workplace.

Workers become anti-union for many reasons—a "bad" experience with your union or another union, dislike of a union personality, warped images fueled by the media, or misconceptions about what the union really can and cannot do.

Whether the reason is legitimate or crazy, you have the opportunity to give that worker a different, positive experience with the union. Since that worker is in trouble and feels vulnerable, she might be more receptive to your message.

So swallow your distaste and try the following:

- Be straightforward and avoid sarcasm in your dealings with the worker. Don't give her any "rope" to hang a duty of fair representation violation on you for treating her differently.

- Explain to her the steps you are taking to handle the case. Make it clear you are handling the case in the same competent way you would handle any other bargaining unit member's case. Keep her informed throughout.

- Involve the worker in the process to reinforce that the union is everyone working cooperatively together. Ask her to obtain information for you and to be with you when you talk to other workers about the case.

- Address her anti-unionism in constructive ways. Probe it and challenge it. For example:

  "Why are you so anti-union?" (Maybe no one has ever asked.)

  "So you had a bad experience once—does that mean all unions are bad?"

  "I've had good experiences and so have Dotty Johnson and Juan Hernandez (other co-workers)."

  "If you think that unions are undemocratic, why would the union try to help you when you are so anti-union?"

- Expect complaints from loyal union members. Explain that the union does not discriminate on any basis—race, gender, ethnic background, religion, sexual orientation or union loyalty.

- If the union wins the grievance, make it a very public victory.

Your actions may not make an instant convert for the union. However, confronted with a positive view of the union, this worker may be less vocal in her criticisms.

At least now you have an experience with that worker to build upon, and you have sent a powerful message to both members and management that the union represents everyone under its agreement.

CONTROLLING THE LOOSE CANNON

A veteran union steward describes a certain species of co-worker this way: "He shoots an arrow into the air, and where it lands he knows not where."

The species being described is the loose cannon. In the world of the union steward, a loose cannon is a well meaning but very individualistic person who acts without thinking. His unpredictable actions can create a life of damage control for the already overworked steward.

Here are some typical loose cannon activities as related by union stewards from across the country:

Enraged by the demeaning way in which a supervisor addressed a co-worker, one loose cannon took it upon himself to express the outrage of the whole union to the supervisor's superior—without the knowledge of the steward or anyone else in the union. The union's position was poorly presented, the ability to file a successful grievance on the issue was damaged, the steward's authority was undercut, the demeaned worker was not made a part of the process. . . . It was a mess from beginning to end.

Another loose cannon urged that the union circulate a petition at her hospital worksite to protest the poor quality of the surgical gloves provided the staff. She volunteered to get the petitions distributed and signed, but once the union provided her with a printed petition to circulate she was already off crusading over a new issue—trash receptacles—and never circulated the petition.

In the middle of contract negotiations, one loose cannon member of the bargaining committee, without consulting with anyone else, wrote letters to the editor of the local newspaper about certain management statements made in the bargaining sessions. Single-handedly, she derailed the entire negotiations.

All these situations point up the dangers of a worker acting on his own in the name of the union.

Loose cannons present a particular dilemma to the steward, because they do possess some valuable characteristics important to building the union. Unfortunately, these positive characteristics come coupled with flaws that can spell disaster.

Loose cannon people are usually energetic and enthusiastic. They like activity and they frequently volunteer. But once the initial surge of an activity dies down, the loose cannons are gone, no longer interested in the routine or follow-up work needed to see a campaign or activity through to the end.

Loose cannons are often intelligent and creative in their ideas, but can lack common sense. They almost always act before they think, leaving a mess behind.

While usually willing to take risks, they sometimes can't see the line between bravery and foolhardiness. While their liveliness and creative ideas attract others to want to work with them, loose cannons are poor team players. Since they flit away from a task once they lose interest, they leave other team members to sweep up the dust of their ideas.

How can a steward deal with a loose cannon? The challenge is to find situations that capitalize on the person's positive traits while avoiding situations that end up causing trouble.

First off, be honest with the person. Describe the effect of his loose cannon activities. Emphasize the importance of the union acting as a united group. Let him know everyone appreciates his positive qualities: energy, enthusiasm, creativity. But emphasize that a union is a team, and good teamwork requires careful planning.

Next, channel the cannons into activities that make effective use of their good energies.

Consider letting them make the union's first contact with new employees; their energy and enthusiasm can give newcomers a good impression of the union.

Involve the cannons in short-term, high-activity projects. On the morning of a rally, for example, ask them to go around and remind co-workers to participate.

If loose cannons can throw you off guard, you can bet they throw management off guard as well. Management is even more wary of them than you are. Use that to the union's advantage when you want to keep the employer guessing. The loose cannon is often good at speaking spontaneously. If you can control the agenda of the meeting, the loose cannon can be effective in a labor-management session called to discuss a particular issue.

Talk through possible scenarios with the loose cannon before an activity. Since loose cannons act before they think, turn the tables on them and make them talk through what they are going to say or do.

The steward who effectively channels the energies of a loose cannon masters an important lesson in union relations—helping people develop their positive attributes and decrease their negative ones.

WORKING WITH TIMID GRIEVANTS

It's usually the worker without a legitimate grievance, champing at the bit to file, pushing you to get in the boss's face, who makes stewards want to tear out their hair. But the flip side of that scenario—the worker who has been unjustly treated but will not come forward—is equally frustrating.

Stewards with their antennae working usually find out when something has happened to a worker. So how do you effectively handle a situation when a worker *should* grieve, but won't?

Let's first look at the reasons such workers do not come forward:

☞ *Fear.* A worker fears retaliation from the boss for speaking up. In today's downsized economy, many workers think they must quietly endure abuse to keep their jobs.

☞ *Guilt.* The worker believes that he did something to provoke the incident. Even if the worker had some role in the incident, the punishment may not fit the crime.

☞ *Shame.* The worker is ashamed of what happened and doesn't want anyone to know. This is common in sexual harassment situations even though the worker has done nothing wrong.

☞ *Ignorance.* The worker doesn't realize that what happened is unjust, or doesn't know that the union can help make things right.

☞ *Cynicism.* The worker doesn't believe that the union can do anything.

When confronted with a timid grievant, it's important to remember that the union—not the individual aggrieved worker—owns

the grievance. Because the union bargains collectively for all the workers in the unit, it must take the action that best protects the interests of everyone. The abuse of one worker, left unchecked because he does not want to file a grievance, could potentially harm others because management likely will repeat the abuse.

Managers sometimes make stewards think that they can't encourage workers to file grievances or that a grievance can't be filed without the signature of the aggrieved worker. Not true. A steward's right to solicit grievances and to file a grievance on behalf of the union are protected activity under National Labor Relations Board rulings.

Here are some suggestions for handling these situations:

- Talk with the worker and find out what happened and why she is reluctant to file a grievance.
- Use that opportunity to reassure the worker that she is not alone. Educate her about her rights. For example, it is an unfair labor practice for a boss to threaten or retaliate against a worker for filing a grievance. Also explain that it is the union's responsibility to protect those rights for all the unit's workers. The union can only be effec-

tive with everyone's participation.
- Explain—particularly to the cynic—your union's record on solving workplace problems. The more participation, the more pressure on management to stay in line.
- Explain that if the union just stands by and lets management get away with the grievance, the worker likely will be targeted again, and the boss will feel free to target other workers too.
- Surely other workers have felt reluctant in the past to file grievances. Have them relate their experiences to the worker.
- If the worker won't budge, determine if there's a better way to solve her problem other than filing a formal grievance. But if filing a grievance turns out to be the best strategy, inform her of that decision.
- Get the entire unit to sign the grievance as a way to both reassure the worker and drive home the message that participating in your union means you are never alone.

Stewards who have developed a high visibility for the union in the workplace by involving others in activities, dealing with workplace issues in creative and fun ways, and firmly dealing with management will remove the barriers that keep workers from coming forward and seeking help if they are treated unjustly.

THE PROBLEM BOSS

Most anyone who has worked for even a few years will tell you that he has had a difficult boss at one time or another. Unreasonable. Grouchy. Petty. Controlling. Arrogant. Short-sighted. Maybe even abusive. A real pain in the anatomy.

Unfortunately, there's no union contract that specifies a boss must be likable. But when a boss is difficult and he or she has little respect for the workers or the contract, your job as a steward becomes even harder.

Let's use some of the Five W's we usually use in grievance investigation to gain a larger perspective on the boss:

1 *Who* **is your boss?** What do you know about this person? What is his background, history with the employer, history as a supervisor? Ask around.

2 *What* **makes your boss difficult?** What specific behavior endangers the contract and adversely affects the workers? That, and not just his unpleasant personality, must be your concern as a steward.

3 *When* **is the boss difficult?** What incidents seem to spark the difficult behavior? When is the boss more even-handed?

4 *Where* **do you stand with the boss?** Is he as difficult with you as with other workers? What approaches can you use given this relationship?

5 *Why* **is the boss difficult?** What pressures is he under? What motivates or influences him? Scratch the surface of a difficult boss and most times you'll find an insecure human being who has poor supervisory skills.

Thinking about and answering these questions, as well as involving co-workers in your investigation, will help all of you get beyond the usual, unhelpful explanation of, "Oh, the boss is just a jerk."

Here are some overall guidelines to help you decide what to do.

PLAY YOUR OWN GAME

Stewards are often tempted to beat the boss at his own game. If the boss is unreasonable, you counter with unreasonable demands. If the boss threatens you, you threaten back. If the boss yells, you yell louder. A more effective strategy is to set your own tone, one that sharply contrasts with the boss's. You're more effective as the calm and reasonable but assertive voice of the union. You are seeking agreement, not conquest. Your job is to enforce the contract, not orchestrate revenge. Your high road approach might even influence the boss to play by your rules, since nobody will play his game.

FOCUS ON THE ISSUE OF FAIRNESS

Make it clear that it is not who is right, it is what is right that counts. When the boss's difficult behavior results in workers being mistreated or losing their rights under the contract, that is unjust and the union won't stand for it. Call the boss on each and every issue of such injustice— again, in a reasonable and assertive way. Use the grievance system for legitimate grievances if you get no satisfaction from verbally trying to resolve it.

SUGGEST ALTERNATIVES IN EVERYBODY'S SELF-INTEREST

Difficult bosses usually operate in an "I must win, you must lose" mode without seeing other options. When the boss's difficult behavior results in a problem, point out to her how another approach could resolve the problem so there's no skin off anyone's nose. As disagreeable as it may

seem, you have to play to some of the boss's legitimate self-interests—and you'll know those from your investigation of the boss's background. The union, too, can't fall victim to playing the "I win, you lose" game.

DEMONSTRATE UNITY

Difficult bosses flourish in places where workers are isolated physically or emotionally. Show the boss that an injury to one *is*

an injury to all by walking into work as a group, eating lunch and taking breaks all together, making it clear you have a telephone tree or some communication system if workers are physically isolated on the job. There are many creative and practical ideas that can back up the rhetoric and discourage the boss from messing with the many.

For you as steward, orchestrating this is also sheer steward survival. You should not continually take on difficult bosses alone—it's ineffective and hazardous to your health.

GO OVER THE BOSS'S HEAD

If you've made efforts to work with the boss and are regularly hitting a brick wall, go to your boss's boss to make your case. Work this out with a union representative to most effectively rattle the chains. Even mediocre managements don't want continued strife in units and find it easier to fire or transfer a first-line supervisor to resolve the problem.

BE OPPORTUNISTIC FOR THE UNION

Difficult bosses are great organizing tools. Channel people's anger and frustration into useful activity. If you're in an open shop, sign up new members in a Workers for a Fair Boss campaign, or some other creative focus. Publicize whatever inroads you do make with the difficult boss.

There are times when ridiculing the boss and making him the issue are appropriate—and some great union campaigns have successfully centered on that strategy. Remember that it is a strategy that has to be very carefully planned with all the risks involved assessed.

For newer stewards, try some of the guidelines suggested here and take comfort that in today's organizations—both public and private—first-line supervisors often have a very short shelf life.

CHALLENGES TO YOUR AUTHORITY

What are the boundaries of a steward's authority and how do you handle challenges to it by supervisors and co-workers?

You have certain rights as a union steward through labor law, your contract and past practices of union-management procedures at your workplace.

THE EQUALITY PRINCIPLE

One of your most important sources of authority is the NLRB's equality principle, which says that when acting in their official union capacity, stewards are not subordinate employees but, rather, equals with their supervisors. As important as the principle is, neither the public nor most workers are aware of it. So, never assume that a supervisor understands your role: management generally does an uneven job of training supervisors on such issues. Usually, *you'll* have to educate them.

MANAGING A SUPERVISOR

Sometimes making it clear that you are the union steward and you are acting in your official capacity clears matters up. Other times you may have to spell out your rights to a supervisor.

Let's say you're interviewing a worker during work time about a possible grievance and are challenged by a supervisor. Respond in an even tone of voice, "As the union steward, I have the right to interview workers on the employer's time." If pressed further, suggest that the supervisor check with his supervisor or with the personnel director on the proper procedures.

Because the equality principle does allow you some latitude in expression in your role as union steward, you'll find an inexperienced supervisor, taken aback by your assertiveness, may challenge you in a grievance hearing when you question his credibility, or when you use confrontational language. Again, it will help to spell out your rights. "As the union steward, I have a right to question the accuracy of your information."

It's also possible that the workers you represent may not fully understand your role. They may challenge you as a busybody when all you are doing is conducting a grievance investigation. When you inform them of the remedies for grievances or outcomes of labor-management meetings they may resist, thinking you are some kind of straw boss.

EXPLAIN YOUR ROLE TO YOUR MEMBERS

Early in your stewardship it is a great idea to sit down with the workers you represent and explain what you can and cannot do. Also tell them what they can expect from you: your best in representing them and how that's done. And let them know what you expect from them: their participation in the union and support for you. From time to time, explain it again for new people on the job.

Sometimes people challenge your authority just to test you—supervisors and members alike, particularly if you are a new steward. Supervisors will want to find out if they can intimidate you. Members want to know if you'll stand up to management, so they'll challenge you first to see how you measure up.

Recognize this experience for what it is.

Stand your ground, keep your sense of humor and you'll pass the test.

Then there's the breed who will challenge your authority just to undermine you. This group includes supervisors who want to dominate and weaken the union's influence, or members with an ax to grind or a personal agenda to push through and who thus want to get you out of the way.

STAND YOUR GROUND

In these situations, you need to stand your ground, getting support from your union representative and, especially, from the others in your unit. Remind them that an attack on you, the steward, is an attack on the union and can threaten everyone.

Your best strategy is always to keep your co-workers well informed and get them involved in what's happening in the union. When you can demonstrate that you have the support of others, you won't have to worry about your authority being regularly challenged.

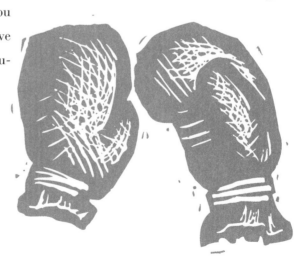

8 THE WORKPLACE AND THE LAW

THE LAW AS A STEWARD'S TOOL/156

You can cite a wide range of legislation—not just union contracts—to help protect your co-workers. Here's a brief summary of some key workplace laws.

THE RIGHT TO REPRESENTATION/158

The law makes clear that workers in trouble have a basic right to have their union steward at their side.

THE RIGHT TO PURSUE GRIEVANCES/160

Workers who file grievances are protected from employer retaliation for doing so, and you can use a variety of tactics to turn up the heat in a grievance fight.

THE RIGHT TO INFORMATION/162

Representatives of the union working to defend the contract have the right to demand a wide range of information from the employer.

WORKPLACE FREEDOM OF SPEECH/166

Guidelines to help you avoid crossing the line between free expression and getting in hot water.

WEARING YOUR VIEWS/167

More and more "message" buttons and T-shirts are showing up in the workplace, and many of them irritate the boss. In a lot of cases, that's just too bad.

LIE DETECTORS IN THE WORKPLACE/169

Ways to respond when management wants to use these untrustworthy devices.

Much of the steward's work consists of serving as an unpaid public defender. While you can't be expected to know all the federal, state and local laws, codes and regulations that affect the workplace, you can begin to learn what they are, and how smart stewards apply them.

That's why this chapter is included—not as a course in the law, but as a way to lose the fear of the law. Remember, it's our law as much as management's, but only if we use it.

THE LAW AS A STEWARD'S TOOL

Too many stewards can't see the forest for the trees.

When a member asks for help to solve a workplace problem, our first instinct is usually to look in the contract. Stewards often think, "If there's contract language, I can file a grievance, otherwise I guess the union can't help out."

But often lost among the trees of specific rights spelled out in the negotiated agreement is the forest of laws and regulations that apply to virtually all workplaces. A union that knows these laws has an option to file a legal action with an outside agency or in court. And since under many contracts we can grieve employer violations of law, not just contract rights, knowing about those statutory rights can give us added clout in arguing a grievance.

Of course, different laws apply to private and public sector employees. But here's a general guide that should help you find your way through the forest of laws and regulations.

HEALTH AND SAFETY

The Occupational Safety and Health Act says employers have a "general duty" to provide a hazard-free work environment, and there are detailed OSHA standards that apply to particular industries and working conditions. Stewards in the private sector have found that one very effective way to get management's attention is to remind them that OSHA has compliance officers who inspect company premises for violations, and can impose fines.

There also are right-to-know laws that can help you find out what chemicals employees are being exposed to, and mandatory OSHA logs, available to you upon request from your employer, that can help you monitor the health and safety situation in your workplace.

UNFAIR LABOR PRACTICES

Workers have the right to engage in a wide range of activities to improve their wages and working conditions. There's legal protection against any employer interference or retaliation when workers do things like join their union, file grievances, wear buttons or T-shirts with union messages, or hand out union literature. And the law says you have extra legal protection the minute you take off your employee hat to do your job as a steward.

DISCRIMINATION

Various federal, state and local laws forbid discrimination against job applicants and current employees based on the following: race, color, age (over forty), sex, religion, national origin, marital or parental status, physical or mental handicap (which includes some cases of drug or alcohol abuse) and sexual orientation. Keep in mind that illegal sex discrimination includes sexual harassment, and that the protection of these laws can extend to discrimination against women who are pregnant.

PLANT CLOSINGS

A number of laws, most notably the 1989 Worker Adjustment and Retraining Notification Act (WARN), require that advance notice be given to unions when a company is planning a shutdown or mass layoff. The law doesn't stop a company from making these business decisions, but the heads-up to the union can give the time needed to organize a community or other campaign to turn the decision around or to bargain a retraining/severance package.

OVERTIME WORK

Laws such as the Fair Labor Standards Act supplement whatever contract provisions we have on the length of the workday/workweek, and overtime pay or comp time. With statutes of limitations measured in years, going outside with such claims can mean real dollars for overworked and underpaid workers, and can be used as leverage to settle a grievance on these subjects.

LEAVE

The Family and Medical Leave Act of 1993 guarantees unpaid leave for workers in a variety of circumstances. While many unions will continue to have better time off provisions in their contracts, the law sets a number of minimum standards, and includes guaranteed health care coverage while a worker is on leave. It also gives returning employees the right to go back to their old jobs or equivalent positions.

Just as important as the laws themselves is the legislation put in place to allow for their enforcement. These rules and regulations establish the basic rights that enable you to legally act as an advocate for workers. In previous chapters we discussed the equality principle. But there are more specific rights that spell out how and when you can be legally present at disciplinary hearings, and how you can represent workers.

THE RIGHT TO REPRESENTATION

One of the most valuable protections a worker has is the right to representation when called in by the boss. A steward's presence as a union advocate can mean the difference between someone being railroaded out of a job and having justice prevail.

Weingarten rights are key when discussing representation. Weingarten rights are named after a landmark 1975 Supreme Court case, *NLRB v. J. Weingarten, Inc.* Through court decisions and legislation, this protection now covers almost all private sector and federal employees and many state and local government employees.

THE WEINGARTEN DECLARATION

For their own protection, workers should be instructed to read or hand this statement to management before the start of any meeting that could lead to discipline:

"If the discussion I am being asked to enter could in any way lead to my discipline or termination or impact my personal working conditions, I ask that a union steward, representative or officer be present. Unless I have this union representation I respectfully choose not to participate in this discussion."

Under Weingarten, in order for a worker to have the legal right to a union representative during a meeting with management, all of the following conditions must be met.

THE MEETING IS AN INVESTIGATORY INTERVIEW

This means that the employee is expected to answer questions in connection with an inquiry into possible wrongdoing or unacceptable behavior. Weingarten rights do not cover meetings where the communication is one way; that is, when the purpose is merely to convey information to an employee or to notify an employee of a decision already made regarding discipline. Keep in mind also that discussions of job performance do not automatically include the right to representation. That right exists only if the meeting also involves giving answers to questions that may then lead to a disciplinary action.

DISCIPLINARY ACTION MAY RESULT FROM THE MEETING

The legal standard here is that a disciplinary action—of any severity—is one possible result of the meeting. Since what matters is whether disciplinary action may result, it legally makes no difference that the supervisor who calls the employee in may not be intending to take disciplinary action.

THE EMPLOYEE REASONABLY BELIEVES THAT DISCIPLINARY ACTION MAY RESULT

The law generally requires only that the employee has a reasonable belief that he or she may be disciplined. Whether that belief is reasonable or not is a judgment call, and will be determined based on all the circumstances surrounding the meeting: Has the supervisor previously raised the possibility of discipline? Have other employees been disciplined for what this individual is accused of? Is this employee working under the threat of a performance warning letter?

A REQUEST IS MADE FOR REPRESENTATION

Weingarten rights differ in one crucial way from the Miranda rights you hear about on television, in which a suspected criminal must be informed of his right to have an attorney, among other things. Unlike the police, employers have no legal obligation to advise workers of their rights before questioning begins. It is up to individual employees to know their rights, and to state that no questions will be answered until a union representative arrives.

Once the steward arrives on the scene, what are the legal guidelines?

☛ *Learn the nature of the investigation.* You can insist on being informed beforehand as to what the questioning is going to be about.

- *Pre-interview consultation.* You and the employee have the right to talk privately before the questioning starts. Use the opportunity to learn what the background facts are, and to give the worker a quick briefing on how best to conduct him or herself during the meeting.

- *Right to participate.* While the employer can insist that the employee give his own account of what happened, you have the right to speak up during the process: to obtain clarification of questions that are unclear, to object to improper questioning and to supplement your answers with other information that may help the employee's "defense."

- *Write it down!* One extremely valuable function you can play is to take careful and complete notes of what goes on at the meeting. This can avoid disputes later on as to who said what.

If a request for representation is turned down and an employee is forced to answer questions, legal relief can be pursued either through a contractual grievance or by filing an unfair labor practice charge with the appropriate federal, state or local labor board.

THE RIGHT TO PURSUE GRIEVANCES

Not only do most contracts guarantee a worker's right to file a grievance, it's a right backed up by the force of law. No one can be hassled or retaliated against for doing what's legal.

Further, you can give more weight to the union's fight for a fair resolution by taking a variety of actions that could lead management to settle the grievance in your favor.

First, a look at some of the ways a grieving worker is protected by law:

- An employer can't make intimidating statements to discourage workers from filing grievances. An example of an illegal action by a supervisor: "Hey stupid, what's the big idea of calling the union?"

- An employer can't retaliate against a worker because he or she files a grievance. Example: changing a worker's shift or giving a less favorable assignment, solely as punishment for filing the grievance.

- An employer can't increase discipline against a worker for filing a grievance. Example: A supervisor tells a worker she's going to be suspended for loafing. The worker says if that's done, she'll file a grievance. The supervisor's response: "File a grievance and I'll fire you."

☞ An employer can't offer special favors—like a management job—to a steward to get him off the company's back. But understand that it's hard to prove such an offer is a bribe rather than a legitimate promotion offer.

☞ An employer can't require a steward to disclose his notes on a case. The relationship between a steward and a worker subject to discipline is confidential, like the lawyer-client relationship.

☞ An employer can't tear up a grievance. The labor board says destroying a grievance in an abusive manner violates the duty to bargain in good faith.

☞ An employer can't refuse to meet with a particular steward. Unions pick their representatives, not management. Union choices must be respected. In the absence of violent or abusive behavior by the steward, an employer violates labor law by refusing to meet.

PUTTING MUSCLE BEHIND YOUR CASE

Not only can't the employer do these things, but the union can undertake other activities in an effort to convince management to resolve the grievance satisfactorily. Under the law, all of the following are acceptable activities. Be sure to get clearance from your union leadership before undertaking some of them.

☞ You can distribute leaflets about the grievance during breaks or before or after work.

☞ You can send a letter to the head of the parent corporation (in the private sector) or the agency head or top elected official (in the public sector).

☞ You can circulate a petition in support of the grievance.

☞ The union can hold a meeting of employees during a break or at mealtime to discuss the grievance.

☞ You can lead a delegation of employees to the labor relations office during a break, carrying signs supporting the grievance.

☞ You can write letters to local newspapers about the grievance.

- In an orderly and nonviolent manner, the union can picket the home of the management person responsible for deciding the grievance.

- As long as the contract doesn't bar such picketing, the union can establish informational picket lines at the workplace. But be sure not to interfere with employees, suppliers or shippers.

- People can wear T-shirts or pins with slogans supporting the grievance.

All of these activities, if sponsored by the union or consistent with the union's position, are protected by labor law. Workers who take part cannot be threatened or punished.

THE RIGHT TO INFORMATION

Pursuing a grievance can be like fighting a war: the more ammunition you have, the better your chances of winning. And one of the best places to get information is from the employer.

Courts generally have held that unions have a right to information—not just so they can bargain effectively, but so they can monitor and enforce the contract as well. The employer's obligation to provide infor-

mation is extremely broad. It includes the disclosure of documents, factual information and data. Management must provide requested materials that could be useful to the union or could lead to the identification of useful information. If the employer doesn't have the information in its possession, it must make a diligent effort to obtain it, including making requests of third parties with whom it has a relationship (such as contractors, customers and parent corporations).

Understand that union requests must be made in good faith, not to harass the employer or to conduct a fishing expedition into the employer's records.

Information requests are good tactics for unions. They help to win grievances and make employers think twice about violating the contract. Information requests should be submitted for almost all grievances.

FACTUAL INFORMATION

Employers must answer pertinent factual questions. For example, in a discharge case, you can ask for all reasons for the discharge and the names and addresses of witnesses who supplied information on which the discharge decision was based. In a subcontracting grievance, you can ask for all sorts of details about the contractor and the work performed.

DATA

Employers must provide you with lists, statistics and data. For example, you can request lists of prior discipline for particular infractions, statistics on pension contributions, or the amounts of bonus payments to employees.

GENERAL INQUIRIES

Unions may make general informational requests such as:

☞ Please supply all documents or records that refer to or reflect the factors causing you to reject this grievance.

☞ Please supply all factual bases for the company's decision.

☞ Please provide all documents relied upon by the employer in the discipline of the employee.

DISCIPLINARY GRIEVANCES

When grieving a warning, suspension or discharge, always request a copy of the grievant's personnel file as well as information about other employees who have committed the same offense. In some cases, you can request information about supervisors and non–bargaining unit employees.

CONTRACT INTERPRETATION GRIEVANCES

If the grievance requires interpretation of contract language, request the employer's notes from relevant bargaining sessions; the dates and contents of any union statements upon which the employer is relying; and the dates and descriptions of any practices or events that the employer contends support its position.

PROMOTION GRIEVANCES

Request the personnel file of the successful bidder, as well as the file of the grievant. Request copies of interview notes and documents evaluating the applicants.

PAST-PRACTICE GRIEVANCES

If you are trying to enforce a past practice, and management contends that the practice is inconsistent, request dates and descriptions of all occasions when management claims a departure from the practice.

HEALTH AND SAFETY GRIEVANCES

If you are grieving an unsafe substance, request a list of workers made sick by the substance, the material safety data sheet (MSDS) supplied by the manufacturer, copies of OSHA or other agency citations, and any studies by the employer concerning the substance. When necessary, the union may arrange for an outside specialist, such as an industrial hygienist, to conduct an inspection of the workplace.

EMPLOYER RESPONSES

Rest assured that employers try many excuses to evade their obligations to supply information. But the National Labor Relations Board has generally denied these. For instance, the NLRB has turned down these employer excuses:

- ☞ The union can get the information from employees.
- ☞ The request is too large.
- ☞ The information has been posted.
- ☞ The grievance is not arbitrable.
- ☞ You can subpoena the information to the arbitration.
- ☞ Past grievances were resolved without this information.
- ☞ The materials are privileged.

There are some areas where the right to information is ambiguous or favors the employer. In most cases, though, the union's rights take precedence. These are the general areas of concern:

Confidentiality Claims

An employer defense that is sometimes successful is confidentiality. This defense can only be used to protect information or records that are particularly sensitive. Employee medical records, psychological data and aptitude test scores are usually considered confidential. Company records disclosing trade secrets or containing sensitive research data have also been deemed confidential. To invoke the confidentiality defense, an employer must have an established policy barring disclosure and must have consistently adhered to that policy.

An employer who asserts confidentiality must be willing to bargain with the union to attempt to accommodate the union's needs. If medical confidentiality is asserted, for example, the union might agree to allow the employer to delete medical references from personnel files or delete employee names. If trade secrecy is raised, the union can offer to sign an agreement promising not to disclose the information.

Time Frames and Deadlines

When it comes to providing data requested by the union, employers are not excused from compliance because of the size of the union's request (although the employer may insist on cost reimbursement). Information requests going back as long as five years have been enforced by the NLRB.

In terms of answering information

requests, there is no uniform deadline. Employers generally must respond promptly but the acceptable time period depends on the amount of information requested and the difficulty in obtaining it. Items such as attendance records should be produced in one or two weeks. Unreasonable delay is just as much a labor law violation as outright refusal.

Filing Charges

The employer's obligation to furnish grievance information runs solely to the union. Individual employees, including grievants, do not have legal standing to file information-request charges at the NLRB. Stewards may file NLRB charges, but should always obtain approval from their chief steward, union president or business agent.

Documents

You are entitled to examine a wide variety of employer documents prior to filing or arguing a grievance. Here are some of the records you can request:

☞ accident reports
☞ attendance records
☞ bargaining notes
☞ bonus records
☞ collective bargaining agreements for other bargaining units or other facilities
☞ company manuals and guidelines
☞ contracts with customers, suppliers and subcontractors
☞ correspondence
☞ customer complaints
☞ customer lists
☞ disciplinary records
☞ equipment specifications
☞ evaluations
☞ inspection records
☞ insurance policies
☞ interview notes
☞ investigative reports
☞ job assignment records
☞ job descriptions
☞ material safety data sheets (MSDSs)
☞ payroll records
☞ personnel files
☞ photographs
☞ piece-rate records
☞ reports and studies
☞ security guard records
☞ security reports
☞ seniority lists
☞ supervisors' notes
☞ time study records
☞ training manuals
☞ videotapes
☞ wage and salary records
☞ work rules

Think of these rights as Freedom of Information, and use them in your interest. Why not? Management does.

WORKPLACE FREEDOM OF SPEECH

It's been said that wisdom is knowing when to speak your mind and when to mind your speech. As you represent your co-workers, a basic understanding of the laws governing slander, coupled with common sense, can save you and your union from potential liability for defamation lawsuits.

The exact definition of defamation varies from state to state. In general, defamation is a statement of "fact" concerning a person that is false, or calls the person's character or abilities into question, and is communicated to a third person.

The statement must be one of fact or suggest that unstated facts support the statement. Statements of opinion do not usually meet this requirement. Distinguishing between fact and opinion may be difficult. One way is to ask if the truth of the statement can be tested or demonstrated. If the answer is yes, the statement is usually one of fact. For example,

courts have ruled that in labor dispute settings, a statement such as "Number-one scab Louise Q. Steinhilber is a jerk" was an opinion.

On the other hand, a job reference stating that an employee's attitude, dependability and quantity of work were merely fair, and the quality of his work was poor, was found by a judge to be a mixed expression of fact and opinion that

the employer implied was based on undisclosed facts.

To defame someone, your statement must be false or substantially inaccurate. For instance, during a labor dispute, the owner of a contracting firm that employed nonunion employees at substandard wages was called "scab." The court concluded that although the statement was unpleasant, it "was literally correct."

THE CHARACTER QUESTION

For a statement to be defamatory, it must call the individual's character or abilities into question. Negative statements about an individual's business or professional reputation, or statements that suggest that an individual is incompetent, dishonest, disloyal or guilty of criminal behavior, are defamatory if they are untrue. Courts have found statements by a union officer calling an employee an informer, stooge, stool pigeon and traitor to the union to be defamatory—the officer couldn't prove the employee was, in fact, an informer.

Courts also said a person was defamed when three hundred employees were informed that he had driven away with company property in his truck without authority—a charge that had not been proven. On the other hand, name-calling or snide remarks about a person's national origin are generally not defamatory. For instance, it was not defamatory for one employee to call another a nut or a screwball.

To be defamatory, the statement must be "published" or communicated to a third person. Courts say that in order to be considered published, the communication must be understood. Therefore, if the speaker communicates in English but the third party understands only Spanish, the statement has not been published.

The best way to avoid defamation suits is to mind your speech. As you represent members, be aggressive. But, be truthful and use common sense. As long as you mind your speech and tell only the truth, you should have no problem.

WEARING YOUR VIEWS

From grassroots issues to pop culture, at rallies and rock concerts, buttons and T-shirts are a fertile medium for self-expression and for showing others where you stand. Employers can disagree with your buttons or insignia, but can they force you to take them off? It depends.

The law on this is controversial and

inconsistent. One thing is clear, however: employers can't ban union insignia simply because they don't like unions. In general, courts protect the wearing of union buttons and shirts as "concerted activity" that must remain free from employer interference. For example, an employer can't allow people to wear political campaign buttons but refuse to let them wear union buttons.

Unfortunately, the law has wavered in defining limits on employer bans. Although it's difficult to generalize, a basic understanding of the law can help you decide when a no-insignia policy goes too far.

☛ To ban union insignia, employers must show "special circumstances." In general, "special circumstances" exist if the insignia disrupt production, cause a safety hazard, incite unrest or alienate customers. The law is fact-specific: legitimacy often turns on the size or color of a button, or the words on a T-shirt.

☛ An employer may prevent workers from displaying union emblems if the emblem could somehow disrupt production or lower product quality. Where the work requires great concentration or sensitive materials, courts have found that the ban rests on a "legitimate business reason." For example, courts have found that a restaurant that forbade food-preparation staff from wearing personal jewelry because of sanitation standards could also forbid wearing union pins.

☛ Courts generally allow bans if the insignia might pose a threat to safety. For instance, if a worker's job puts him in contact with flammable mate-

rials, the employer may legitimately prohibit him from wearing paper decals on a helmet or jacket. Of course, an employer must enforce its ban uniformly: if the rule bars union decals it must also bar equally flammable decals that aren't union-oriented.

☛ Employers may ban emblems that contain controversial messages that might "incite unrest." It's unclear whether the employer must show that the emblems actually cause problems, or just have the potential to cause problems. For instance, if a strike has caused violence between workers, an employer can prevent returning strikers from wearing No Scabs buttons as a precautionary measure. On the other hand, the employer may not use this excuse to prevent workers from wearing pro-union insignia during a peaceful organizing drive. Courts also allow bans on T-shirts rapping the company's product or containing obscenities.

☛ The possible alienation of customers may also justify an employer's ban on pro-union articles. The level of customer contact, type of business and conspicuousness of the union emblems are all factors. For example, courts have allowed wholesale bans on "unauthorized" adornments where employees wore strict uniforms and the company projected a "uniform public image." In contrast, though, courts have struck down similar blanket prohibitions by clothing stores or health care facilities because the bans unreasonably applied to workers who had no contact with the public.

There are no absolute rules for determining when special circumstances exist, but an employer might be able to make a ban be enforced if it falls into one of these loose categories. If not, however, the ban is illegal and the employer may not discipline, discharge, discriminate or threaten employees for displaying pro-union insignia.

LIE DETECTORS IN THE WORKPLACE

"Who knows what evil lurks in the hearts of men?" asked the old radio show, *The Shadow*. Armed with a polygraph machine—a so-called lie detector—employers imagine that they can unlock the innermost secrets of the human mind, scientifically discovering truth and falsehood.

Although federal and state laws severely limit employers' use of polygraph tests, many companies and government agencies continue to subject workers to the anxiety and humiliation of these supposedly scientific examinations.

Despite the name, a lie detector is not able to detect a lie. It is simply a machine that measures certain changes in the body's reactions, such as blood pressure, pulse, breath rate and perspiration.

The basic theory behind the polygraph machine is that the act of telling a lie causes a person's body to react in measurable ways. The obvious problem with this theory is that these same bodily responses— sweating, heartbeat, blood pressure—are affected by all kinds of stimuli, not just lying. Scientific research, certified by the American Psychological Association and the congressional Office of Technology Assessment, has concluded that it is impossible to tell if a polygraph exam can accurately distinguish truth from lies.

Under federal law, no private employer (except security and pharmaceutical companies) can directly or indirectly require a worker to submit to a polygraph test as a condition of employment. It is illegal to fire, discipline or discriminate against a worker for refusing to take a polygraph test or for complaining about polygraph testing.

However, the boss can lawfully ask a worker to submit to a polygraph examination under limited circumstances.

Specifically, if the test is part of the employer's ongoing investigation into a theft or similar economic loss, and the employer has reasonable suspicion that the worker was involved in the theft, and the employer has given the worker a written statement detailing the grounds for suspecting him.

If a worker is asked to undergo a polygraph test, he or she must be given a written notice of the time and date and nature of the test, and has the right to see the test questions before the test is given. The test cannot include questions of a personal nature. The worker has the right to consult with an attorney, and to stop the test at any time during the exam.

A worker cannot be tested if he has proof of any medical treatment that could affect the polygraph results. Also, the test must last at least ninety minutes, to give the

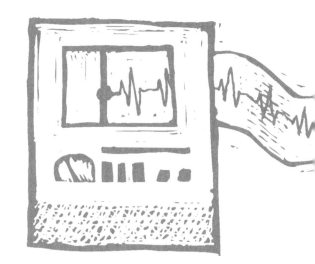

worker time to adjust to the stress of being hooked up to a machine.

In order to protect workers from needless harassment and unjust discipline, the steward should demand information from the employer concerning the justification for testing a worker. In addition to the written statement required by law, the steward should ask for any backup information, such as statements by any witnesses.

The steward should also insist on information about the test itself, such as the list of questions to be asked, and a copy of the test results. Since the test results reflect the subjective judgments of the person administering the test, it is important to determine the qualifications of that person.

Of course, as always, the worker has the right to have a union representative present during any interrogation. The steward should be prepared to stop the examination if inappropriate questions are asked.

Finally, the steward must know the contract. The law does not preempt any prohibition or restrictions on polygraph tests included in the collective bargaining agreement.

9 TAKE GOOD CARE OF YOURSELF, BABY

MANAGING YOUR TIME/174
Some simple ways to keep the demands on your time under control.

TAMING THE TELEPHONE MONSTER/176
A few tips on how to keep the phone from eating your life.

DEALING WITH STEWARDS' STRESS/177
Stress comes with the territory, but there are ways to keep it from driving you up the wall.

Much of a steward's life is determined by events outside his or her control. You can't keep people from filing trivial grievances, improve a boss's personality or insist that problems be limited to just one a week. But there are still many things you can do to make problems more manageable and less of a drain on your time and emotions.

Consider these techniques and give them a try. You might be able to avoid a few unnecessary headaches and maybe even an ulcer or two.

MANAGING YOUR TIME

It's a fact of life for stewards: there's always too much to do, never enough time. You know your work for the union is important—but does it have to consume your life?

Take heart. There are some practical actions you can take right now to make your life easier and more manageable.

SET PRIORITIES AND STICK TO THEM

Go through your steward's workload and decide what's important and what's not. Decide, too, what's most urgent, and what can wait. Then go after the urgent and important jobs first: for example, grievances with time limits.

Next, give your energy to tasks that are important but not necessarily urgent. For example, organizing your files may seem like one of those jobs that could be put on a back burner, but chances are you'll find yourself way ahead when you're finally able to locate information quickly when you need it. Conversely, if you spend all your time putting out little fires—dealing with matters that are urgent but not important—you can end up even further behind.

WRITE IT DOWN

Many stewards use a pocket-sized notebook and calendar to keep track of priorities, especially grievance deadlines. There's a lot more your notebook can do for you if you get into the habit of writing everything down: what's said in phone calls you make or receive, ideas for letters you need to write, insights into workplace problems, questions you're asked and may need to research, and so on. By taking notes on everything important, you ensure that your work gets done, and you also get rid of that nagging feeling that you're forgetting something crucial.

COMBINE TASKS WHENEVER POSSIBLE

If you've just begun to process several

grievances, for example, try to do the research on all of them at one time. Then write all the necessary letters or fill out relevant forms for all the grievances at once.

If you need to call another union official for any reason, think about any other questions for that person that may come up in the next several weeks and get all the information you need in one phone call.

If you travel routinely to different departments or worksites, perhaps you should arrange your filing system accordingly, so you'll be able to check in one place on all the problems and grievances pending at each location before you visit.

GIVE YOURSELF SPACE

Whatever your load as steward, you're going to need space to work, to write and to file necessary paperwork. Some stewards may be able to get desk space at their workplace, especially if they have the contractual right to perform union duties while on the clock. Another solution is to set up an office at home—not necessarily a whole room, but at a minimum a desk or table, filing system and perhaps even a phone you can use for your union work. Once you've got a spot, use it, and keep all union-related notes and papers in the place you've set aside.

SET A SCHEDULE

If your efforts for the union tend to take up time outside working hours, you may want to create a strict schedule for those efforts and stick to it. For example, you could set aside an hour a day, after work, to deal with phone calls and paperwork. Whatever time you allow, you want to make union work a regular but limited part of your life.

TAMING THE TELEPHONE MONSTER

The telephone can be the biggest time-grabber of all. If you can manage to reduce the amount of needless time spent on the phone, you're far ahead of most trained managers—and that's one place worth being.

Try these proven techniques:

- Plan each call before you dial. Take a minute to think about the purpose of each call you make. You may want to get a specific answer to a question, or set up a meeting, or have someone mail you information.

- Before you make the call, jot down the results you want. Then, as you talk, make notes not only on what the other person says, but also of your own responses.

- When you hang up, you'll not only have a record of that call, but can also create a follow-up letter, if necessary, that you may want to send to confirm any decisions that were made during the call.

- Set a time limit for each call at its beginning. If you are making the call, begin by saying something like, "I've only got a few minutes, and I wanted to check one point with you...." When someone calls you, tell them at the beginning of the call that your time is very limited by saying, "I'm glad you reached me. I've only got five minutes"—or whatever amount of time you want to commit.

- Short-circuit the endless call. Sometimes people can't or won't accept your statement about having limited time. Many people also have trouble finding ways to say goodbye. If you're talking to one of these people, first restate your time constraint. Then summarize your conversation. "You've told me about this problem you're having—is there anything else?" Briefly state what you plan to do about the issue that's been put before you. If you will need to talk to that caller again, set up a definite date and time. "I'll discuss your situation with . . . (the supervisor, another union officer, etc.) and get back to you by _____." Then end the call.

- Don't play telephone tag. This time-wasting game begins when you make a call, find that person out and leave a message that you called. They call back but you're out. And on and on. This is a growing problem, thanks to the increase in the use of voicemail systems. End the game by leaving a specific time when you can be reached. For example, instead of leaving a message, "Have Ann Smith call me back," say "I need to talk to Ann Smith before 3 p.m. today, when I'm leaving, so please have her call me about the pending grievance as quickly as she can."

DEALING WITH STEWARDS' STRESS

Even if you use time-management techniques you may still feel frustrated and overwhelmed on occasion. Emergencies and unplanned events can set you back. You may find yourself consumed by fear, worry or physical responses that just plain make you want to scream. What follows are a few ways to begin to cope with these unwelcome responses and put yourself on the right path.

For starters, when stewards talk about "all the stress" they're feeling at work, they usually mean *dis*-stress—a condition that many of us feel too much of the time. In fact, the physical and emotional health problems directly related to dis-stress have become so common that stress is now referred to as the disease of our era.

STEVE MAGNUSON

How did this happen? To better understand this all-too-common modern ailment, it helps to know about the body's fight-or-flight response. This is something we're born with, a birthright given to all mobile creatures—whether they want it or not.

HOW THE BODY PREPARES FOR FIGHT OR FLIGHT

☛ The brain mobilizes the body for vigorous action

☛ Pupils dilate

☛ Mouth goes dry

☛ Neck and shoulder muscles tense

☛ Breathing is faster/gasping

☛ Heart pumps faster

☛ Blood pressure rises

☛ Liver releases glucose to provide energy for muscles

☛ Adrenaline and other hormones are released

☛ Muscles tense for action

☛ Digestion slows down or ceases

☛ Sweating begins

☛ Sphincter closes

THE FIGHT-OR-FLIGHT RESPONSE

Our ancient ancestors needed this emergency body reaction, this shot of adrenaline, in order to escape the daily onslaught of wild animals, hostile neighbors and other deadly dangers.

The good news is that this effective emergency response helped the human race survive. The bad news, however, is that our bodies still kick into this kind of response today, but with much less provocation (for example, a verbally abusive boss, a member of the union who you catch working off the clock, or a child who's out past curfew). In fact, unless we use counter-measures to reduce stress, we can pump as much adrenaline into our systems while trying to meet a work deadline as our ancestors did while fleeing from a hungry lion.

Unfortunately, this inefficient, outdated system can, over time, produce constant wear and tear on our bodies.

On the other hand, there's good news. There are ways to rewire our minds and bodies so that they don't automatically over-react to our daily, non-life-threatening dilemmas.

A key to good physical and mental health is keeping a balance between positive stress and dis-stress. Imagine for a moment that you are a musician who plays a stringed instrument—let's say a six-string guitar. The

SOME DISORDERS THAT MAY BE RELATED TO EXCESS STRESS

Headaches, dizziness, insomnia	Excessive sugar in blood
Blurred vision	Backache
Difficulty in swallowing	Nervous rash
Aching neck muscles	Allergies
High blood pressure/cardiovascular disorders	Excessive sweating
Over-breathing, asthma, palpitations	Mucous colitis
Indigestion, ulcers	Sexual difficulties

strings must have some tension in them if they're to make any sound at all. If they're even a little too loose, they will sound flat, dull. However, if they're wound too tightly they will sound sharp and could even snap in two when played.

To help you maintain this kind of delicate balance, try making these changes in attitude and approach.

CHANGE THE WAY YOU RESPOND

You may not be able to make stress go away, but you can alter the way you think about it. Research has shown that people who persist in negative views of events usually experience more stress than people who concentrate on positive elements. Focus on your strengths, and try to see your job as a challenge.

LEARN PROBLEM-SOLVING SKILLS

Think of your stress as a puzzle and find ways to solve it. If something really bothers you, try collecting all the information you can about the situation and develop a plan of action. For example, if the same kind of grievance keeps coming up, think about strategies to deal with the underlying problem that is causing the grievances to surface again and again.

MAINTAIN EMOTIONAL DISTANCE

It's easy to feel overwhelmed by another person's pain—especially when you may know that person well. But you can provide the most help, and also protect yourself, by listening to people's problems with detached concern.

EXERCISE

This advice may seem too simple—but it's been medically proven that a twenty-minute aerobic workout three times a week will release muscle tension and drain away the hormones our bodies produce in stress situations. Find an exercise you enjoy and stick to it.

TURN TO OTHER PEOPLE

Create a support network. Family members, friends and other union officers and stewards can offer not only a sympathetic ear when you feel overwhelmed but also may have concrete and helpful suggestions on how to handle a particular problem. Don't hesitate to ask for help from other stewards or officers in your union; chances are someone else has confronted the same kind of problem in the past and may be able to tell you exactly what to do.

Go beyond the workplace. Reaching out to friends and family, joining community associations, the PTA, a church—even getting a pet—are all ways to fight back.

THE FOUR-COUNT BREATH

Another method is the Four-Count Breath. Here's how it works: By slowing down and regulating your breath, you can signal the brain that you were only kidding when you first sounded the alarm for the fight-or-flight response. It's a little like throwing a switch that moves a speeding train onto a track that will force it to slow down. The deliberately slowed breath will in turn cause the heart to slow down, the blood

pressure to stabilize and the muscles to relax. A particular beauty of this technique is that you can do it anywhere, anytime.

Here's a good way to learn the Four-Count Breath:

If possible, sit in a comfortable position with your back straight, your hands relaxed and resting in your lap. Begin by simply noticing your breath—how fast you're breathing, how deeply. Just notice—don't change it. Next let all the air out of your lungs, exhaling slowly, deeply. As you inhale, silently count a slow but comfortably paced "one-two-three-four." Then exhale, again counting to yourself "one-two-three-four." As you exhale, you can also "exhale" all the muscle tension in your face, jaw, neck and shoulders. Repeat this process over and over until you feel quiet and calm. That's all there is to it.

As thoughts come into your mind, simply notice them and return your attention to the breath and the count. One great benefit of doing this simple breath count is that it can slow down your racing, repetitive and/or negative thoughts.

Try this technique a few times to see how it works for you.

LAUGH A LOT

No situation is so solemn or serious that you can't find a way to poke fun at it if you try. Stretch your sense of humor with joke books, cartoons and videotapes.

And for the final word on stress relief, consider this philosophy of life, offered by legendary pitcher Satchel Paige, who stayed in the major leagues until he was forty-seven years old:

> Avoid fried meats which angry up the blood. If your stomach disputes you, lie down and pacify it with cool thoughts. Keep the juices flowing by jangling around gently as you move. Go very lightly on the vices, such as carrying on in society. The social ramble ain't restful. Avoid running at all times. Don't look back. Something might be gaining on you.

WHEN ALL ELSE FAILS, GIVE IN

In the end, though, you'll have to accept your limitations. Even Super Steward couldn't handle every part of your job perfectly. Admit that you make mistakes, that you have had and will have bad days, even bad weeks. As one psychologist has written, "If you can't flee and you can't fight, flow."

10 SPECIAL ISSUES

It would make life a little easier for stewards if all the important workplace issues fit neatly into categories such as contract, legal and interpersonal. But some of the problems and issues stewards are faced with just don't fit into easy compartments.

On occasion, stewards will find themselves having to defend not only the contract but the union itself and even the entire labor movement, warts and all. Anti-union workers and management will want to hold you personally responsible for any mistake—real or invented—that unions make.

At other times stewards will find themselves having to deal with hot-button issues like race and gender—difficult, often emotional, potentially divisive issues that can affect an entire workplace.

And at still other times stewards are called on to help in situations that involve medical or other health concerns. After all, more than 40 million Americans deal with one or more legally recognized disabilities, and untold millions contend with alcohol or drug problems. These are issues that don't stay confined to workers' homes.

This chapter offers advice and counsel on dealing with some of the different ways your skills will be stretched as you carry out your steward duties.

THE "DEATH" OF UNIONS

Every so often, the media produces new reports on the "death" of unionism. Anti-union sentiments flourish in every part of the country, and corporations and other groups that oppose unions feed on such reports.

That's why union activists need to know how to answer all those anti-union arguments. You've got to fight back with the facts. Here are some ideas about how to rebut the most common complaints about unions.

UNIONS: GREEDY?

Corporations traditionally blame unions not only for rising prices of consumer goods, but also for plant shutdowns and the decline of entire industries. But most experts disagree, pointing to many factors, including bad management decisions, that led to our current trade and economic problems.

One proof that unions are not to blame is the fact that American companies—union and nonunion alike—are losing business to highly unionized companies in other countries. Germany, Japan and even Singapore have higher rates of unionization than the United States, and some American companies have lost business to them. North

American employers, especially since the 1994 approval of the North American Free Trade Agreement, also are taking jobs to low-wage areas like Mexico and other Latin American countries, as well as Asia. In many of these countries it's not a question of paying union wages, or even nonunion wages, by North American standards. It's a question of paying 20 cents or 50 cents or a dollar an hour, with little or no environmental or other controls.

If people want to talk about greed, they should consider this: according to the *Wall Street Journal*, in the mid-1970s the average chief executive officer of a major company was paid 41 times what his average employee got. By the early 1990s the gap had increased to 225 times more.

UNIONS: INFLEXIBLE?

Many people believe that unions' rigid rules about seniority and distribution of work have led to American industrial decline. The truth is that unionized companies are much more likely than nonunion firms to experiment with teamwork, self-management and other innovative practices.

Researchers find that unions support these programs for two important reasons. First, unions usually gain something in return for relaxed work rules—such as improved job security, profit sharing or higher wages. Second, union leaders also know that participatory programs give workers more options to improve working conditions.

UNIONS: CORRUPT?

It's true that a few union leaders have been convicted of illegal activity, but the vast majority of union leaders are honest and hard-working. They have to be: unions are one of the most democratic institutions in America.

One study found that within a two-year period, about three-quarters of the membership went to at least one union meeting and about the same percentage voted in a union election. Several studies show considerable turnover of union leaders at all levels.

And union leaders' failings, such as they are, are nothing compared to what goes on in American business. A survey of more than one thousand companies a few years ago revealed that 11 percent of them were involved in major crimes such as bribery, tax evasion or criminal fraud.

Unions clean up their corruption problems smack in the public eye, as every newspaper reader knows. Corporations, on the other hand, can usually bury their problems in the boardroom.

UNIONS: SPECIAL INTEREST GROUP?

Of all the anti-union arguments, this is the weakest. Look at what unions have done for all Americans. Union support helped pass laws to achieve social security, public education, unemployment compensation, civil rights, voting rights and worker safety. Today, unions continue to fight for health care for everybody.

By tearing apart all these anti-union arguments, you reveal a simple truth: unions are good for American workers. Unionized workers not only earn about one-third more on average than nonunion, but they also have more job security, health benefits, pensions and protection against unjustified discipline.

HANDLING DUES COMPLAINTS AND FREE RIDERS

There's no getting around it: most members don't like to pay dues. To many, dues are just another deduction from their paycheck, no different from federal or state or city taxes, no different than sales taxes or use taxes or any other tax.

Of course, people who stop to think

about it see that taxes pay for the highways they drive on and the police who protect them and the schools that educate their children. Taxes help assure that the water their families drink is pure and the food they buy at the market is safe to eat.

But people *don't* stop to think about it, no more than as union members they consider how, without dues, there would be no lost-time pay for bargaining committee members, no funds for training, no lawyers to pursue arbitrations, no one to turn to when they're unfairly docked or disciplined, no trained representatives to take their side when things get bad. They would be at the mercy of their employers—and an awful lot of employers show no mercy whatsoever.

So how does a steward deal with the member who pays his or her dues or agency shop fee but gripes about it nonstop? How does a steward in a "right-to-work" situation convince people to join and stick with the union?

You could consider offering these thoughts next time the issue comes up.

MAKE THE COMPARISON BETWEEN TAXES AND DUES

People may not like paying taxes, but without them there would be no roads. People still drive on those roads, though, and couldn't function without them. Likewise, they still count on the firefighters to respond if their house or apartment burns. They *use the services* that tax monies support, even though they're not crazy about taxes. Likewise, they *benefit* from the union's work, even though they might not like paying the dues that make the union's work possible.

LIST THE BENEFITS

If they don't like paying dues, then presumably they don't like the very things that dues *bring*: job security, raises, vacations, health insurance and pensions. Examine your contract, and next time someone starts on about "those damn union dues" be prepared to list some of the benefits that wouldn't exist without the union.

COMPARE AND CONTRAST

Do some legwork and study up on wages, hours and conditions at another employer—a *nonunion* employer—in your community, one that could reasonably be compared to your own in terms of the kinds of jobs people do. Be prepared to show your members what the job protections and wage and benefit differences are between the two, and make it clear that the union—and thus *dues*—are the reasons for those differences. Maybe you can even get your hands on a paycheck stub from the other workplace, and show it as evidence.

STEVE MAGNUSON

GIVE THEM SOME STATISTICS

In the United States, average union pay in 1995 was $5,241 a year higher than average nonunion pay. Union-negotiated benefits are even more dramatic: a whopping $7,571 higher, according to the Bureau of Labor Statistics. AFL-CIO economist John Zalusky did some calculations and found that the wage and benefit difference is so great that the monetary return on a union card is eighteen times the cost of union dues. Put another way, for every dollar you invest in dues, you get $18 back.

USE THE REFUND TECHNIQUE

Next time some loudmouth starts spouting off about dues, especially in a break room or other place where there are a lot of workers around, just say something like: "Gee, I'm so sorry to hear you're unhappy with the union. Here: I'll give you back your dues money, right out of my own pocket."

Reach into your pocket and count out a few bills. You'll have everybody's attention.

As you're holding the money, say something like, "Of course, I'll need something in return. Since you're so displeased with the union and want nothing to do with it, I will need you to sign a form saying that in exchange for getting your dues money back from me, you will give me in return any benefits the union has negotiated for you."

The member will probably be a little surprised at this point and say something like, "What do you mean?"

Your response should be along the lines of: "Nothing really. Just things like when you get a paid vacation or holiday that's in the contract, you don't get the pay, I do. And next month, when our employer has to pay for your health insurance, the money will go to me instead. And of course you'll have to give me the difference between the minimum wage and what the union has negotiated." And so forth.

At this point the member is usually willing to look a little more reasonably at the question of dues—and the discussion has been an education for all the other members in the room.

USE THE BALANCE SHEET TECHNIQUE

Prepare a sheet that adds up the dollar value of union-won benefits. Health insurance is worth so many dollars over the course of a year; paid vacation is worth so many dollars; pensions, bereavement leave and so on. Add up all those numbers, and then add up the cost of union dues. Then subtract the dues from the total value of the benefits the worker receives, and you've got an impressive bottom line.

You might be able to handle things in a different way, but your goal is to have members or potential members add up the actual cash value of their union contract, and compare that to the cost of union dues. In every case the cost of dues will be insignificant in comparison with the dollar value of what workers gain through the union's work.

BUILDING UNITY IN A DIVERSE WORKFORCE

The U.S. Department of Labor projects that by the year 2000, more than five out of every six people entering the American workforce will be women, immigrants and people of color. For a lot of stewards, this statistic can add up to a real challenge.

Why? Because being a union steward can already have you dealing with expressions of powerlessness, divisiveness and conflict—attitudes and problems that tend to be an everyday part of life, especially at work. Working in an ethnically diverse setting can add even more challenges, and it can be useful to develop some understandings and aids for helping people work together, and work out their differences.

Here are some hints for how to think about team building in an increasingly diverse workforce.

DEALING WITH APATHY

Experiences of discrimination or bigotry often leave people feeling powerless and mistrustful. Those feelings can get communicated through expressions of apathy. Workers may say they don't care about an issue or they don't want to get involved, but what they often really mean is they don't know what to do to remedy the situation.

Giving people skills to figure out how to resolve their problems gives them a sense of power. For example, both the expressions of apathy and the feelings of powerlessness can frequently be short-circuited by showing how to use the very real collective power of their union and their union contract. It's amazing how a victory or two will change people's attitudes about themselves, their co-workers and their ability to make a difference.

Any conflict, whether it's between supervisor and worker or workers themselves, will have at least two parts: the actual problem and the emotions surrounding that problem. In helping people work through their conflict, it's very useful to keep those two elements—the emotions and the actual problem—separate. This can be done in several ways.

For one, you can try giving people a separate space where they can be listened to as they vent their emotions, without being concerned at the moment about either resolving the problem or even sounding rational. Then, when the emotions have been vented and the people involved have cooled down a bit, you can look at the problem itself. If the parties start getting back into the emotions at this point, they've already vented the worst of it and it's a little easier to direct them back to the problem at hand.

SORTING OUT KEY ISSUES OF A CONFLICT

Wading through the often confusing mass of issues that a conflict may generate can be made easier in a number of ways. Here are some strategies and principles to keep in mind the next time you try to mediate a conflict among people of different races, ethnicities or sexes:

☛ Get to what's underneath the prejudice. This can be thought of as the "ouch" beneath the comment or behavior. For example, someone says, "You just can't trust those people, they're all alike." You could respond with, "It sounds like you've had some bad experiences. What happened to make you not trust them?" This response marks you as a person willing to listen and it opens the door for

a real dialogue.

☛ Lift the level of discussion and assist the person to think about the whole problem of racism and sexism in our society. Racist and sexist comments are unthinking and can often be short-circuited by inviting a person to think with you. For example, if someone tells you a racist or sexist joke you could respond by asking them to think with you about why there are all these uncomplimentary jokes about people of color or women. Keep in mind that while they may seem harmless, racial and sexual jokes really do create a climate that breeds insensitivity and bad feelings.

☛ You can ask the parties to a conflict to outline their position, while you listen to each side without interruption. If the parties are together, this noninterruption procedure will have to be agreed to at the start. Keep notes on the underlying concerns of the parties' respective positions. If the parties are together during this process, you should list concerns in a way that everyone can see them. By listing the concerns, you and the parties can begin to determine what concerns are held in common, and you can start to explore broader ways of framing the issues so that both sides' real interests are taken into account.

☞ Remember, reducing prejudice around you requires the courage to intervene. That may mean being targeted yourself, but in the long run it also means you build a stronger and more united group. Principled leadership empowers others to be principled, even those you might least expect.

THE VICTIM/VICTIMIZER ROLES

Often, when we think about discrimination or bigotry, we think about two roles—the victim and the victimizer. We tend to think that some of us are victims and some are victimizers: for example, the worker as victim and boss as victimizer. Unfortunately, it is not always that simple. We *all* play both roles, at different times and in different places.

For example, a white worker can certainly be victimized by economic oppression, with bosses and managers as the victimizers—but that same white worker can in turn be the agent of racism in relation to an African-American. What is even more interesting, though, is that even when we

are acting in bigoted ways we don't usually *experience* it as such. Strange as it sounds, we usually experience it as *ourselves* being victimized. A good example is the male worker who defends his comment that a woman's place is in the home by voicing the fear that *they* (women) will take jobs from *us* (men).

It's useful to understand that feelings of victimization are at the very base of attitudes and behaviors that hurt and divide people. So, at least in part, *defusing* these attitudes and behaviors means healing those feelings of victimization, and it means helping the person recover her or his real sense of power.

For example, in some political campaigns, white workers have been manipulated into believing they will lose their jobs if an African-American is elected to Congress. This kind of manipulation can be short-circuited by really listening to how people feel insecure and fearful. If you listen well enough, provide correct information, and pose questions in a way that encourages people to think, you can often bring about some real change and empowerment. One question you could ask: "It sounds like you care a lot about people getting a fair deal. What do you think we can do to make sure white workers are not set up against black workers to achieve that end?"

THE DISUNITY ARGUMENT

At a Welcoming Diversity Workshop at the AFL-CIO's George Meany Center for Labor Studies, one of the participants raised the fear that looking at "all this diversity stuff" would completely destroy what little unity the labor movement often seems to have.

It's an understandable fear, one that can be used as a defense for such comments as "Why can't they just fit in and not make such a big deal about who they are? Aren't we all just Americans?" Again, acknowledging this as a fear and hearing people out is the first step. For example: "Yeah, I know that it can be pretty scary to think that this could really divide us even more, and it sounds like our unity is really important to you. Tell me more about how you see it."

Lastly, as we fight our battles around wages, benefits and other issues, it's important that the big picture of what we're really fighting for be presented: if we don't, people can get manipulated and set against one another. This picture should include the fact that racism, sexism, homophobia and the like are used to keep working people divided and unable to fight their true foes. The goal here is to end the way our relationships with one another are exploited and to reclaim the value of that wonderful old principle, all for one and one for all.

Understanding the dynamics of how people are separated from one another and learning strategies for healing those rifts are key to building a group of people who can fight for one another's rights.

RESPONDING TO SEXUAL HARASSMENT ISSUES

Marjorie refused her supervisor's date invitations and suddenly it seems all the better assignments are going to other people. When Marjorie asks him about it, he tells her she hasn't adequately demonstrated "teamwork skills" to obtain these assignments.

The men at Kathy's workplace put up *Playboy* pinups in the break room. Kathy has never heard them refer to the pictures or make sexual remarks to women on the job, but she feels humiliated by the pictures.

What should stewards do about the situations these women face?

POWER

Incidents involving sexual harassment are particularly challenging. The incidents involve strong emotions, misuse of power, and the tension that historically surrounds relations between men and women in our society.

Unions have an obligation to make sure that all members are sensitive to the problem of sexual harassment in the workplace, and to create an environment in which victims of harassment will feel comfortable turning to someone in the union for assistance.

The steward must investigate claims of sexual harassment as thoroughly and seriously as he or she would investigate any other grievance claim. Additionally, the steward must be sensitive to the victim. Victims—and most sexual harassment victims are women—often feel anxious, powerless, shamed and guilty. Confidential hearings for victims and the accused might be the best first step.

LEGALITY

To be effective, it's important for a steward to know what legally constitutes sexual harassment.

Briefly, sexual harassment is any unwelcome sexual advance, request for sexual favors, or any other verbal or physical conduct of a sexual nature.

Because of the law, sexual harassment is grievable even if your contract doesn't have specific language about it. So stewards should use their grievance procedures as one strong way of dealing with sexual harassment situations.

Marjorie's case—she "hadn't adequately demonstrated teamwork skills"—is the classic form of sexual harassment. In such cases, a superior tries to sexually coerce a subordinate through implied or direct threats of losing a job or promotion or getting less desirable assignments.

The supervisor most likely will deny he made advances. Undoubtedly, he will blame the employee's work performance or cite management rights as his justification for the change.

HISTORIES

The steward should ask management to document anything that is alleged about the employee's work performance. The steward should also interview others in the department to see if this supervisor has a history of harassment; frequently harassers do, although no one may have complained before.

Employers are more likely than ever to treat these grievances seriously, because the courts have made it clear that management is responsible and liable for the actions of its employees. Ignorance of the situation cannot be used as an excuse.

ENVIRONMENT

Kathy's case, with the pinups, involves work environment. It's a category of sexual harassment that is less clear cut than Marjorie's. It's also more sensitive for the steward, since it's Kathy's co-workers—possibly other union members—who have put up the offensive pictures. However, legally, the employer still bears the responsibility for the atmosphere of the workplace because he allows it.

In a case like Kathy's, the steward should warn her co-workers that even if the pictures offend only one person, they're offensive and have no place at work. While it's not the steward's job to discipline workers, it is his or her job to warn them about possible consequences of their actions. Continuation will undoubtedly lead to management disciplining workers over it, since management is ultimately liable.

PREVENTION

Stewards should be prepared to take some static from co-workers who will claim that their behavior is in "good fun" or that workers like Kathy "just can't take it." You could remind such co-workers that if Kathy

was their daughter, wife, mother or sister, they wouldn't want her treated like that.

The best strategy for dealing with the issue is a preventive one—educating workers about the issue before incidents occur.

Stewards should give the following advice to workers if they experience sexual harassment:

- ☞ Complain immediately to someone in the union.
- ☞ Tell the offender very firmly that the behavior is unwelcome and offensive and that you want it to stop immediately.
- ☞ Keep a written record of events: what exactly was said; when; where; and names of witnesses. Record what you said in return, and how you felt.
- ☞ Seek support from friends, family and the union. No one experiencing harassment should have to endure that alone, and the steward plays the key role in demonstrating that the union is a supportive and discrimination-free organization.

DEALING WITH GAY AND LESBIAN ISSUES

It's a new day out there. With more and more people coming out, gay, lesbian and bisexual members are an increasingly visible segment of the labor movement. The AFL-CIO and many individual unions have issued policy statements strongly endorsing equal rights for gay and lesbian workers.

Is there a role for shop stewards to play? Are sexual orientation issues union issues at all? Here's why fair-minded unionists think so:

☞ A union member is a union member is a union member. Race, sex, age, sexual orientation . . . they make no difference. Every dues-paying member deserves just as much of the union's support and protection as every *other* dues-paying member.

☞ The proudest moments in union history have been when we've said that justice issues—like civil rights for racial minorities—are union issues, too. And often unions are the only ones who can fight for the rights of gay and lesbian members. While the Canadian Human Rights Act outlaws discrimination based on sexual orientation, on-the-job discrimination in the United States is still legal in more than forty states.

☞ Gays and lesbians may not be as numerous or visible as some other groups of members—like women or blacks—but that doesn't lessen their right to representation. *All* union members deserve union representation in dealing with workplace concerns.

☞ The oldest management trick in the book is divide and conquer—whether it's along lines of race, sex or sexual orientation. When we unify all workers we build union strength. If you've got a fight with management on your hands, it's senseless not to try to get *all* of your members involved.

Here are some practical ways stewards can build workers' power by acting on gay and lesbian issues.

IDENTIFY AND ORGANIZE AROUND THE ISSUES

Since you are the union's eyes and ears in the workplace, one of your jobs is to alert union leaders to the issues your members want addressed in contract negotiations. You might want to raise as items for bargaining such issues as adding sexual orientation to your contract's nondiscrimination language, extending health care coverage to domestic partners, and expanding bereavement or sick leave. If your contract already has nondiscrimination language, make it clear to management and to your members that you stand ready to enforce it vigorously.

EDUCATE YOURSELF . . . AND YOUR CO-WORKERS

You may need to make a point of learning about the workplace needs of this segment of your membership. Stewards who are not familiar with gay and lesbian workplace issues shouldn't hesitate to ask "out" co-workers for help. If you need training on how to deal with gay and lesbian issues, get it. A lot of unions have gay and lesbian caucuses: that's a good place to start.

PUSH FOR A HARASSMENT-FREE WORKPLACE

Gay and lesbian members have the same right as female and nonwhite members to a working environment free of derogatory comments and attitudes. Stewards can set an example by using language that does not exclude gays and lesbians: think about how such a person would feel if the first words out of your mouth upon meeting are, "So, are you married?" And don't stand by and do nothing when someone does or says something

offensive; speak up! Just as with sexual harassment of women or racial harassment of minorities in the workplace, your silence sends a message that you—and the union— tolerate unfair treatment.

ENCOURAGE *EVERYONE'S* INVOLVEMENT

These are union issues. Make sure that gay and lesbian issues in your workplace are *acted on* as union issues. Think about it: we don't expect female members to tackle sex discrimination on their own. Nor would we *think* of telling a member in a wheelchair to fight for an access ramp on his or her own. So why assume that straight members wouldn't be involved in making the workplace more fair to gay and lesbian workers?

The bottom line? To be effective in organizing the unorganized and mobilizing the already organized, we can't afford to ignore the needs of *any* population group.

HELPING DRUG AND ALCOHOL ABUSERS

Union stewards wear a lot of hats. Not only do you ride herd on the contract to make sure that the members' basic rights are protected, but you frequently find yourself as the workplace sage who knows a lot, who even plays a parental role in watching out for your workmates.

Rarely does that role take on more importance than when a co-worker has a substance abuse problem. This is serious stuff: it can destroy the worker's life. In some settings, it can even put at risk the jobs or lives of people around them.

Because confrontation is hard, many of us find ourselves denying that the people around us may be in trouble with alcohol or drugs. Also, some of us may feel that substance abusers should take responsibility for their own problems, and their problems should not involve us.

Since substance abusers themselves generally deny the problem, unless stewards and co-workers face it, the odds are it will eventually be dealt with by management—perhaps by termination.

HOW CAN YOU TELL WHEN SOMEONE'S IN TROUBLE WITH ALCOHOL OR DRUGS?

Unless a substance abuser reports to work grossly intoxicated or high—which is not the usual scenario—there are other signs to look for. These signs are most valid when observed over an extended period of time.

Performance Deteriorates and Absenteeism Increases

☛ Inconsistent quality of work and overall lowered productivity.

☛ Increased mistakes, carelessness and errors in judgment.

☛ Absenteeism and lateness accelerate, particularly before and after weekends. Excuses are often vague and confusing.

☛ Unexplained disappearances from the job occur more often.

Attitude and Physical Appearance Changes

☛ Work details are neglected and assignments are handled sloppily.

☛ There's a lack of willingness to take responsibility—others are blamed for the individual's shortcomings.

☛ Personal appearance and ability to get along with others deteriorate.

☛ Co-workers often show signs of poor morale, usually as a result of frustration from covering up for the substance abuser.

Health and Safety Hazards Increase

☛ A higher-than-average accident rate becomes apparent.

- Needless risks are taken in order to raise productivity following periods of low achievement.
- Safety of co-workers is often disregarded.

HOW CAN YOU TALK WITH A TROUBLED CO-WORKER?

Although substance abusing employees may be very angry and defensive on the issue, it's possible for stewards and co-workers to address the problem of substance abuse directly with them. The key: take a stand that is assertive, but not angry, and absolutely honest. Directly state the facts as you have observed them by describing the person's behavior while at work. Be very honest about your feelings, especially in how their abuse has affected you. Assure them that you will no longer get caught up in covering up for them, because this approach has done little to help them, and has not alleviated the problem. In fact, in many ways, it has enabled the problem to continue.

If an Employee Assistance Program is available, strongly urge the individual to make an appointment with a counselor. Tell the worker you will accompany him if he wants. If there is no EAP, do your homework ahead of time by calling your union's membership service office or the National Council on Alcoholism and Drug Dependency (800-622-2255) to determine the available resources for help. Have a list of these resources when you confront the employee so that concrete suggestions and offers of help can be provided.

When all else fails, and you see a truly dangerous situation, stewards and co-workers in workplaces where the union contract guarantees job protections for troubled workers can consider a difficult, but potentially life-saving alternative. That is, step up the pressure on a substance abusing co-worker by consulting with an understanding supervisor or some other sympathetic person in a position of power. You could save a life—or more than one.

It is wise to remember that even though these actions are uncomfortable and difficult, the overall goal is to help the abuser break through his denial and seek help, before he seriously hurts himself or a co-worker. Your honesty and willingness to be direct may be just the thing that convinces the abuser to change his behavior, and consequently, change his life . . . and maybe that of his or her co-workers.

STEWARDS AND DISABLED WORKERS

Since it took effect in July 1992, the Americans with Disabilities Act of 1990—a landmark civil rights law—has revolutionized the workplace by extending the civil rights umbrella to cover people with disabilities.

Modeled after the landmark Civil Rights Act of 1964, the Americans with Disabilities Act (ADA) provides equal opportunity in employment to workers with disabilities. Essentially, the law says that if a worker is qualified, an employer with fifteen or more employees may not refuse to hire that worker because of his or her disability. It has the potential of providing significant benefits for workers across the country, providing union representatives with an additional tool for effectively fighting for members' rights.

Although many workers have been fearful of the ADA, it has, in fact, required the updating of job descriptions and job requirements in a way that can actually be helpful. Properly written job descriptions and requirements:

☛ will make jobs available for disabled members that can be performed while their physical or mental health improves, or give them continued employment;

☛ outline clear, job-related factors on which selection and promotion decisions are based;

☛ provide guidelines for measuring skill, effort and responsibility for pay purposes;

☛ eliminate unrealistic skill and responsibility barriers to promotion; and

☛ develop reasonable workloads for all.

Here are some key points about the ADA, along with some suggestions on how to educate your members and how to effectively deal with management on disability issues.

The ADA requires employers and unions to provide people who have disabilities with equal access to services and to ensure they are accorded equal opportunity in hiring.

DEFINING DISABILITY

A person with a disability is broadly defined under the ADA as someone "who has a physical or mental impairment" such as blindness, epilepsy, diabetes or cerebral palsy "that substantially limits one or more of the major life activities." It also covers anyone with a physiological disorder, disfigurement or condition; emotional or mental illness or learning disability; or a person who is HIV positive. A person with a documented record of impairment is protected, as is someone who is generally regarded as having an impairment.

Another protection is that employers may require a medical exam only after an offer of employment has been made and before the employee begins work, and only if all workers are subjected to the same exam regardless of disability.

Once hired, businesses are required to "reasonably accommodate" employees with disabilities as long as the accommodation does not cause "undue hardship"—a term relating to the expense an employer may encounter while making modifications. Undue hardship also refers to the level of disruption to the workplace: that means violating the terms of a collective bargaining agreement, in order to make a reasonable accommodation for a worker, might be considered an undue hardship.

A reasonable accommodation means making adjustments such as widening a door frame to accommodate a wheelchair, installing a ramp, or hiring an interpreter for a deaf person.

Most adjustments won't bankrupt a business; according to a study at the time of the legislation's passage, half of all accommodations for employees with disabilities

cost less than $100.

Stewards should understand that meetings, training sessions, conferences and social events must now be conducted at facilities that can accommodate all workers with disabilities. Sometimes this will mean changing where meetings are held. It can mean building ramps for wheelchairs, or hiring a sign language interpreter for the hearing impaired.

Employees with disabilities must be accorded equal access to whatever medical plan is offered to the other, nondisabled employees.

QUALIFICATIONS AND ESSENTIAL FUNCTIONS

Under disability law, to be qualified to handle a job, a person should be able to satisfy skill, experience and other job-related requirements, and should be able to perform the job's essential functions, with or without reasonable accommodations.

Employers must identify a job's functions—the absolute basics required. Marginal tasks, described as "other duties as may be required by management," are excluded. Since many job descriptions are outdated or were poorly written in the beginning, a new description of essential requirements may uncover elements of skill, experience, effort or working conditions that were initially overlooked and might justify a higher wage rate.

THE ATTITUDE BARRIER

Often, the biggest barrier that workers with disabilities face is other people's negative attitudes or erroneous images of them as helpless, sick victims.

These paternalistic and demeaning attitudes cause many to hide their disabilities and suffer hardship for it. Some medical conditions are not easily apparent—a worker who must sit and rest after only a short walk due to a heart condition, for example, or a worker who has been diagnosed HIV positive.

In dealing with these issues, stewards must try to create an environment where workers feel comfortable explaining their disability. Explain to them that they have a right to recourse if their workplace is inaccessible. And help to educate your co-workers.

☞ Take the opportunity to get to know your union brothers and sisters with disabilities. Barriers and myths continue to exist because of lack of personal experience and fear of the unknown.

☞ Use common sense—treat co-workers like everyone else.

☞ Offer assistance—ask if they would like help. If declined, don't persist; often assistance will be requested.

☞ Create a committee—consider establishing a new workplace committee, including people with disabilities, to deal with issues of accommodating workers and implementing changes.

AN OPPORTUNITY FOR THE UNION

The law underscores the need to keep job descriptions up to date. This provides the union with an opportunity to secure more objective data on job description components such as:

☞ Physical requirements, including work posture, repetition and weight handled.

☞ Mental effort required in specific jobs.

☞ Information on working conditions, including exposure to heat, noise, fumes, chemicals, allergens and other undesirable factors making life difficult.

☞ Realistic education, training and experience requirements.

Understand this: the intention of disability law is to give people with physical or mental disabilities an opportunity to be promoted or hired if they can perform the work with only a reasonable accommodation. A union and employer can continue to base promotions, transfers, work assignments, shift preferences, overtime and other conditions relating to work performance on understandings reached through collective bargaining.

Stewards need not be afraid of disability laws. If anything, they provide a means by which disabled union members can be assured of a job, because the law requires employers to make reasonable accommodations so they can continue to work. Now, employers are required to set up reasonable qualifications that may not have been properly spelled out before.

COUNSELING ON MEDICAL CLAIMS

Some employers, wanting to prevent abuse and fraud, are often overzealous in reducing or denying sickness and disability benefits and leaves for on-the-job illnesses and injuries. Although contracts and disability plans differ, a sharp steward may help a member increase his or her chances of receiving benefits by being aware of the following procedures. Keep two things in mind, though. First, the extent to which claimants need to go to satisfy employers varies considerably from workplace to workplace, and you normally shouldn't

have to go to some of the extremes outlined here. Second, you don't want to volunteer information *not* requested by the employer, because you can set an unreasonable precedent for other claimants.

DO SOME GROUNDWORK

For starters, before filing benefits claims, both the claimant and his doctor should have a clear understanding of the claimant's job duties. The best source to assist them is the employer's job description, a copy of which should be given to the doctor. This will make it easier for doctors to adequately articulate to the employer how the injury or illness relates to the job duties. Doctors frequently do not understand the duties and functions involved in a job, so they don't know which information is essential for payment of employee benefits.

THE IMPORTANCE OF MEDICAL REPORTS

The claimant should provide the employer with a clear statement from his attending physician(s) describing how his present medical status has prevented and/or will prevent him from being at work. Offering the employer even a detailed doctor's statement of the symptoms, diagnosis and return-to-work date may not be sufficient. Employers routinely reject claims on the basis of insufficient documentation even though they have not made the doctors aware of deficiencies in their medical reports, nor told them what was needed and expected.

The documentation should cite which job duties cannot be performed and why. If working aggravates the condition, the doctor should report specifically what about the work worsens the condition.

Whenever possible, get the doctor to document objective findings—findings that can be observed from tests such as x-rays or CAT scans, as opposed to subjective findings (such as pain and headaches), which cannot be determined and proven to exist by any testing.

TREAT THE CONDITION AGGRESSIVELY

Claimants should see their physician(s) regularly and follow a relatively aggressive treatment strategy. If appropriate to the illness or injury, claimants should also be prepared to use some form of physical therapy, psychotherapy or rehabilitation in addition to medication to improve their condition and meet the employer's expectations.

The treating doctor should be urged to set a definite date for the claimant to either return to work or return for treatment. Medical status reports should evaluate the claimant's medical status in relation to his job duties, assess the progress of current treatment and consider if, and what type of, future treatment may be necessary. The employee would also be well advised to acquire a specialist's opinion, which will carry much more weight with the employer than that of a general practitioner.

COOPERATION CAN HELP

To avoid a battle over benefits, the claimant should comply with employer requests such as submitting medical documentation in a timely manner, checking in with a supervisor periodically, seeing a doctor who works for the employer and/or seeing an independent doctor. This information allows the employer to possibly place workers in less physically demanding jobs or to modify the duties of their former job. An employee who attempts to work in other positions, and conveys to the employer his seriousness about returning to work, is more likely to receive benefits. In some cases, the employee may want to take the job under protest and later file a grievance. In all cases, however, the employee should demonstrate good faith.

STAY OFF THE SKI SLOPES!

Many employers will keep a close watch on claimants if the claim adds up to a lot of money—even to the point of hiring private investigators to videotape the worker away from the job. However, simply because an employee may perform a certain act at home a couple of times in a day does not necessarily mean that he can perform the same act repeatedly at work all day long. Still, an employee should ensure that his lifestyle at home and at work are consistent with one another, and with his medical limitations, and return to work when he is again able to perform the functions of his job.

DEALING WITH WORKPLACE DRUG TESTING

Irresponsible drug or alcohol use is destructive, and it can lead to disaster at work—not just for the abuser, but for those who work with the abuser or whose lives count on his job performance. At the same time, however, just because drug and alcohol abuse is a major problem in today's society, that doesn't give employers a free hand to do whatever they want on the issue.

The big thing among employers these days is testing, and stewards should be aware that the law isn't open-ended. A private sector employer cannot impose drug testing on an organized workforce without negotiating with the union: drug testing as a condition of employment is a mandatory subject of bargaining. (The situation is somewhat different in the public sector, where employers generally have more latitude but constitutional right-to-privacy issues are still being debated.)

Some private sector employers attempting to impose drug testing have claimed that the tests are required by the Drug Free Workplace Act of 1988. Not true. The Drug Free Workplace Act requires that government contractors establish drug awareness programs and other efforts to discourage drug abuse, but does *not* require any employer to test workers for drugs.

Stewards should be aware that the most common types of drug tests being used by employers involve chemical analysis of urine. These tests can never show whether a person is currently under the influence of drugs. Urine tests can only indicate whether a person has ingested drugs at some point in the past, since the chemicals that show up in urine are metabolites, the chemicals created by the body's reaction to the drug. Thus there is technically no way for urinalysis to indicate whether the worker was impaired by drug use on the job, or had been exposed to the drugs off-duty, days or even weeks earlier.

When the boss demands that a worker submit to a drug test, the steward, as a representative of the union, has the right to demand information concerning the basis for the test, the test procedures and any possible consequences of the test. The steward can help protect the worker's rights and prepare for any challenge to subsequent disciplinary action by getting answers to these questions:

☛ Does the collective bargaining agreement explicitly permit drug testing? Is there any rule against off-duty drug or alcohol use?

☛ Is there reasonable cause to suspect the worker of drug use, such as evidence of erratic behavior? Has the employer explained to the worker the consequences of refusing to take the test, or of testing positive?

☛ Will the test be administered on employer time? Is the union steward allowed to be present during the testing? Will the worker be required to sign any form of waiver relieving the employer of liability for the test?

☛ Has the worker been offered the opportunity to explain his or her suspicious conduct, or to take sick leave instead of submitting to the test? Has the worker been exposed to any substances such as herbal teas, poppy seeds or prescription or over-the-counter medications that might cause false positive results?

☛ Is the worker going to be observed while giving the urine sample? What are the qualifications of the person collecting the urine sample? Will the employer and the testing laboratory maintain a proper chain of custody?

☛ Who will receive the test results? Will the test results be kept confidential, like any other medical record?

Finally, the union can arrange to have the worker promptly submit to another independent drug test by medical personnel selected by the union.

RESPONDING TO WORKPLACE SMOKING CONFLICTS

Life is getting increasingly tough for smokers in today's workplaces. In the public sector, many recent state and local laws and ordinances have totally banned smoking inside buildings. In the private sector, employers are revising or implementing rules that either ban smoking outright or limit the practice to small areas located away from nonsmoking employees.

The steward is in the middle, and has to try to help both groups of employees—smokers and nonsmokers—cope with the new reality.

So, what do you do? What kind of solutions can you work out? What can you expect if a smoking issue ends up in the hands of an arbitrator?

MANAGEMENT'S RIGHTS

First off, keep in mind that management usually has the right to unilaterally issue work rules. In almost all recently published arbitration decisions on smoking, arbitrators have nailed down the boss's right to issue reasonable rules provided he gives employees timely notice. Arbitrators *do* expect to find some evidence that the union was contacted in advance and had an opportunity to state its opinions. And arbitrators don't like employer-wide bans that even include outdoor areas where health hazards from secondhand smoke are minimal. The lesson here? By settling for a designated smoking area, the union can take care of its smoking membership. In one workplace, a smoking zone in a central area became the most popular meeting place frequented by both smokers and nonsmokers.

Arbitrators generally consider health and safety concerns a good reason to ban smoking in work areas. Medical authorities agree that smoking is bad for your health, and arbitrators uphold smoking bans for this reason. What unions can do is work with management for the creation of well-ventilated smoking areas that don't threaten nonsmokers, and try to get management to allow smoking outside, near entrances and doorways.

THE PAST-PRACTICE TRAP

Don't make the mistake of thinking an arbitrator will rule with smokers because smoking has been a condoned past practice. Current information clearly establishes that smoking is a health hazard, and arbitrators have been upholding management rules. At the same time, though, workers should not have to expose themselves to winter winds just to have a smoke during breaks. The steward should try to get management to recognize that smokers ought to have the option to continue smoking, at least at break time, and a place ought to be provided for them.

Unions that have pursued the "refusal to bargain" tactic to fight new smoking rules have found that the ploy doesn't seem to work. Arbitrators always consider publishing work rules to be a management right unless modified by the agreement.

As usual, your best friend is your negotiated contract. If you have a clause that sets forth smoking areas or the right to smoke, you're in good shape. The only problem your members have is to be sure that they conform to the terms of the agreement. If you have a smoking rights clause, then management is obligated to negotiate with the union before changing its policy.

DUE PROCESS HELPS

Keep in mind that arbitrators tend to support due process issues (notification of rule, clearly stated penalties, careful investigation and consistent treatment of all employees covered by the rule). And discharge for a first offense of smoking in a nonsmoking area was judged by one arbitrator to be too severe where no one else's health or safety was endangered by the act. Stewards have to explain the discipline

rules to the employees and be prepared to protect workers if they have not been given due process called for by the rules.

Employers get sympathy from arbitrators when they argue that they have a business interest that is improved by no-smoking rules. At the same time, though, arbitrators tend to support smoking in designated areas, either inside or out, during breaks and lunch hours. The steward's job is to make sure that the employer's concern for productivity can be documented.

Stewards need to protect smoking workers from unfair discipline. They need to work with management to create safe smoking areas, and they should at least secure for smokers the right to smoke during breaks when productivity is not impaired. It's a tough job for stewards, because while the smokers need your help, you have just as much responsibility to nonsmokers to protect their right to a smoke-free environment.

RESPONDING TO SHORT-TERM SUSPENSIONS

Employees are often reluctant to file grievances over short-term suspensions. After all, compared to a discharge, a suspension seems to result in relatively little harm. And a lot of employees don't want to appear as if they're troublemakers. Instead of fighting it, some workers will laugh off a suspension, saying, "Hey, I wanted a couple of extra days off, anyway."

But a smart steward never allows a suspension to go unchallenged. Accepting the suspension without a fight sets a precedent for *other* employee suspensions based on the same issue. More important, though, today's suspension could help contribute to tomorrow's termination. The reality is that the presence of a suspension on an employee's record may directly result in an arbitrator's decision to uphold that employee's discharge on a similar or related issue sometime in the future.

In deciding whether to uphold an employee's discharge, arbitrators routinely place great emphasis on the employee's disciplinary record and on the employer's use of progressive discipline. That means the presence of a suspension on an employee's record can play a big role in an arbitrator's determination on whether or not to uphold a discharge. Arbitrators look at an employee's disciplinary record like a judge looks at a newly convicted criminal's rap sheet to decide what kind of sentence to hand down.

If an employee has already been suspended once, therefore, an employer will have an advantage at a subsequent arbitration of that employee's discharge: the record will show that the worker is a problem. So, looking down the road a bit, suspension grievances can be as important to an employee's job security as discharge grievances.

Stewards must challenge suspensions when they happen and not wait until the employer discharges the suspended employee. Suspensions must be grieved in a timely manner because, as a rule, arbitrators will not allow belated challenges of suspensions—challenges that come only in the course of a later discharge arbitration.

For example, say the union files a grievance challenging the discharge of an employee who received a two-day suspension one year before his discharge. If the union did not originally challenge this suspension within the contract's time limits, an arbitrator at the discharge arbitration will not allow the union to argue that the suspension was unjust.

If the affected employee is reluctant to fight a "mere" suspension, stewards must make sure the worker understands that what looks like a relatively minor punishment today can contribute to job loss down the road.

Still, the union and the employee may agree that they want to challenge the suspension only if the employee is later discharged. If that happens, the union can inform management that it is withdrawing that grievance without prejudice to a future challenge of the suspension. That means the union is withdrawing the grievance, but is reserving the right to argue the merits of the suspension at a later date, if necessary.

By withdrawing the grievance without prejudice, the union is informing the employer that, despite its unhappiness with the discipline, it does not plan to take the matter to arbitration at that time. If the suspended employee is later discharged, however, the union can then challenge both forms of discipline. Remember, though, an arbitrator will only allow a later challenge to the suspension if the suspension grievance is on record as having been withdrawn without prejudice.

As a final note, if you do file a grievance challenging an employee's suspension, and if the employer discharges the employee while the suspension grievance is still pending, grieve the discharge, but do not ignore the suspension grievance. You must continue to process the suspension grievance in a timely manner in order to preserve the union's right to challenge the suspension in addition to the discharge. The discharge grievance *will not* automatically incorporate the pending suspension grievance.

For example, in one recent case, an employer denied an employee's suspension grievance at the second step of the grievance process. Shortly after denying the suspension grievance, the employer discharged the employee. The union thought that the grievance it filed to challenge the discharge incorporated the unresolved suspension grievance, so it focused all its efforts on the discharge grievance and ignored the suspension grievance.

When the union took the discharge grievance to arbitration, the arbitrator refused to let the union challenge the suspension. The arbitrator said the union had never appealed the employer's second-step denial of the suspension grievance. He decided that the suspension grievance was not incorporated in the discharge grievance (1) because the discharge grievance did not mention the suspension and (2) because there was no express or written agreement to merge the two grievances.

Consequently, the union must process suspension and discharge grievances independently unless the union and the employer expressly agree to consolidate the two grievances. To consolidate a suspension grievance with a subsequent discharge grievance, a steward should refer to the suspension in the discharge grievance and should get a written consolidation agreement from the employer.

AGENCY SHOP   A workplace in which not all employees are required to join the union as a condition of employment, but those who don't must pay the union a service fee equal to dues. Most common in the public sector.

ARBITRATION   A method of settling grievances in which the union and the employer agree to have a neutral third party resolve the conflict. In some public sector and transportation industry settings arbitration can be ordered by the government. The arbitrator's decision is final and binding on both sides.

BARGAINING UNIT   A group of workers who negotiate collectively with their employer through their union, and who are covered by a single union contract.

CHECK-OFF   A system of dues collection in which the employer agrees to deduct union dues from members' paychecks and forward the money to the union. In some unions the money goes to national or regional headquarters; a portion is sent to the local union. In other unions it works the other way around.

COLLECTIVE BARGAINING   Negotiations between representatives of the union and the employer to work out an agreement on wages, fringe benefits, hours and working conditions. Most successful collective bargaining activity results in a contract that lasts a specified number of years.

CONCERTED ACTIVITY   Action taken by workers for mutual aid or protection. Such activity is protected by federal labor law.

CONCILIATION (OR MEDIATION)   A process in which the union and the employer agree to have a neutral third party try to help the two sides resolve a dispute, frequently the inability to agree on a new collective bargaining agreement. Unlike arbitration, the conciliator's decision is not binding on the two sides.

CONTRACT (OR AGREEMENT)   The legally binding document worked out in collective bargaining between union and employer, usually covering wages, benefits, hours and working conditions, as well as procedures to resolve grievances or other disputes that may arise. By signing the contract, labor and management agree to abide by its terms.

CONTRACT LANGUAGE The specific wording found in the contract. Differences in what specific words mean, and how language in different parts of the contract may appear to conflict, frequently lead to arbitrations.

DISCRIMINATION Treating one worker differently from another because of race, age, national origin, religion, sex, sexual orientation or union membership.

FAIR REPRESENTATION, DUTY OF (DFR) The legal duty of a union to fairly and equally represent every employee in a bargaining unit, regardless of whether the employee is a union member. Federal labor law says that unions that do not represent a worker fairly can be charged with an unfair labor practice or sued.

FREE RIDER A worker in an open shop who does not join the union, even though he or she is enjoying the same negotiated wages and benefits as the member who pays dues to finance the union's work.

FRINGE BENEFITS Benefits to workers other than wages that are contained in the union contract. They include things like health insurance, sick days, and vacations and holidays paid for in whole or part by the employer.

GRIEVANCE Any violation of an employee's rights on the job, usually because of the employer's failure to live up to contract language. Grievances can also be caused by an employer's violation of laws or its own management policies. Most contracts contain language about the process both sides use to resolve grievances. The final step in the grievance process is usually arbitration.

GRIEVANT A worker who files a grievance through the union, or a worker for whom the union files a grievance.

MEDIATION *See* Conciliation.

MOBILIZE To bring workers together to help the union achieve a goal, as in mobilizing the members during contract negotiations to show that they are in support of the union's demands.

NATIONAL LABOR RELATIONS BOARD (NLRB) The enforcement arm for the National Labor Relations Act (sometimes called the Wagner Act, or the NLRA). The NLRA was enacted in

1935 and guarantees workers in the private sector the right to "engage in concerted activities for the purpose of collective bargaining or other mutual aid or protection."

OCCUPATIONAL SAFETY AND HEALTH ACT

A federal law passed in 1970 "to assure as far as possible every working man and woman in the nation safe and healthful working conditions." The act created the Occupational Safety and Health Administration (OSHA) within the Department of Labor to set and enforce workplace health and safety standards.

OPEN SHOP A worksite in which union membership is not required as a condition of employment. This is the situation in twenty-one "right-to-work" states and in many public sector worksites. *See also* Free rider.

PAST PRACTICE The way things have traditionally been done in a workplace. Even if the practice is not specified in the labor-management agreement, the union can grieve if management attempts to make a unilateral change.

PRECEDENT A decision or existing practice that is used as a rule or guide for later decisions.

"RIGHT-TO-WORK" LAWS A term used by opponents of unions to describe state laws banning the union shop and other maintenance-of-membership contract clauses. Union supporters often speak of them as "right-to-work-for-less" laws. Twenty-one states have such laws.

SCAB (OR STRIKEBREAKER) An employee who reports to work, or an outsider who accepts employment, even though the workers are on strike. By helping the employer continue his operation, scabs weaken strikers' chances of winning their fight.

SENIORITY A worker's length of service with an employer relative to the length of service of other workers. Contracts frequently use seniority to determine layoffs, promotions, recalls and transfers.

SHIFT An employee's work schedule, as in day shift, night shift or overnight shift.

STEWARD (ALSO SHOP STEWARD, COMMITTEEMAN OR GRIEVANCE HANDLER) A

union activist appointed by union leadership or elected by co-workers who represents a specific group of co-workers and the union in union duties, grievance matters and other employment issues.

STRIKE A temporary stoppage of work by a group of employees to show how serious they take a grievance or demand for changes. Most commonly comes at the last stage of collective bargaining, when the union will not accept the employer's proposed contract and the employer will not accept the union's.

UNFAIR LABOR PRACTICE A violation of the National Labor Relations Act. Legal charges concerning unfair labor practices are filed with the National Labor Relations Board, which can hold hearings on complaints and assess penalties against violators.

UNION SHOP A workplace in which the contract calls for all employees to be members of the union.

WEINGARTEN RIGHTS The right of a worker to union representation when being questioned by management on a matter that could result in disciplinary action. The worker must ask for such representation; the employer is not required to tell the worker of his rights. The term derives from a 1975 U.S. Supreme Court decision.

WORKERS' COMPENSATION An insurance system established by state law throughout the country to provide financial benefits to workers hurt or injured on the job. Under law, workers may not sue their employers over workplace injuries.

INDEX

SUBSCRIBE TO STEWARD UPDATE NEWSLETTER

The source for most of the material in *The Union Steward's Complete Guide* is *Steward Update* newsletter, published six times a year since 1989 by Union Communication Services, Inc., of Washington, D.C. and Annapolis, MD. More than 1,000 local unions and councils across North America subscribe to the newsletter today on behalf of their stewards. ● The minimum order is 20 copies, at an annual cost of $227. Additional stewards can be served for an additional $5 per steward per year. Spanish-language copies are available at the same prices. ● Unions may order by calling 1-800-321-2545, by visiting our World Wide Web site at www.unionist.com or by returning the form below by mail or fax.

ORDERING INFORMATION

❑ Begin my union's one-year subscription for $227. I understand we will receive 20 copies of *Steward Update*, six times a year. (Please note if some or all copies should be in Spanish.)

❑ We have more than 20 stewards and need additional copies. The no. of extra copies we need of each issue is _____

You can order by phone by calling UCS, Inc.
at (410) 626-1400 or call toll-free: 1-800-321-2545;
or by faxing an order to: (410) 626-1353.
E-mail: unioncomm@compuserve.com
Website: www.unionist.com

Subscription (20 copies) $ 227
Additional copies @ $5 each $_____
Total $_____

NAME	
TITLE	
UNION (INTERNATIONAL & LOCAL)	
ADDRESS	
CITY	
STATE	ZIP
PHONE	

CHECK ENCLOSED ❑	VISA ❑	MASTERCARD ❑	AMERICAN EXPRESS ❑	BILL ME ❑

CARD NO.	EXP. DATE

CARDHOLDER'S SIGNATURE

Mail to: UCS Inc., 165 Conduit Street, Annapolis, MD 21401